Abled in A Disabled World

By Evin B. Hartsell

Abled In A Disabled World

ISBN 978-1-7325036-2-5

Request for information should be addressed to:

Curry Brothers Marketing and Publishing Group

P.O. Box 247 Haymarket, VA 20168

Cover design: Nellie Crichlow

Table of Contents

FOREWORD

I truly miss my brother. Everyone in our lives fills a part of us that we do not truly see until that part is gone. The part I realized that I missed most was the engaging conversations that Evin and I would share. Evin's conversations were engaging, thought provoking, justifying, and even to some extent infuriating, but never boring.

Evin and I grew up among avid conversationalists. One of our fondest memories centered around a great debate between our uncles over the gun control rights. While our other cousins were content to run around outside and play, Evin and I just sat and watched, wide eyed, as these two grown men battled one another with their thoughts and ideas.

This was the relationship that Evin and I shared so often on my visits home, and what I missed most. We would debate one another on any topic and under any circumstance. We would attempt to challenge the very nature of the world in which we lived. It was Evin's way of engaging and helping the world. For us, it was both a game and it was serious, but always with a mutual respect and love for one another. Well, maybe it could have been done with a little more love. It was during one of these late night discussions, three years before Evin passed away, that we were discussing the challenges that he had to face. For almost all of my life, I was a witness to and participant in the struggles of Evin's life: from pushing his wheelchair up a steep ramp into the car, carrying him up the stairs, helping to feed him and even taking him to the bathroom.

This night however, I genuinely realized how Evin must have felt to be the one being pushed or carried or fed. While I would never venture to say I could fully appreciate his personal challenges, I couldn't help but be inspired by Evin's journey. So that evening I recommended that he write out his life story so others might see what I saw. That evening began the concept and vision of this books outline. Evin way unable to write by himself due to his physical challenges, but that never stopped him from accomplishing his goal of trying to help others by writing his book. Over the next several months, Evin would either speak into a voice recorder or call me to type out his thoughts. As I became more invested in my career, I was compelled to pull back from assisting him, but I was encouraged to find out that Evin continued telling his story just the same.

It is incredible to think that Evin achieved what he set out to accomplish in writing this book. I am certain that as you read his journey you may find yourself engaged, provoked, amused, saddened, angered or even inspired. But one thing is sure when Evin is involved, it will certainly not be boring.

Alex Hartsell

Introduction

"I am the same as you. I just look different."

Do me a favor. Imagine what it's like to be a physically disabled person like me. First, sit down in an armchair, maybe a dining room or office armchair. Rest your arms on the arms of the chair, put your feet down flat on the floor and sit with your back against the back of the chair. Pretend that your body is smaller and skinnier and that your arms and legs are really wasted. Now bend your wrists backward. Keeping your arms in place, bend your chest all the way to the right and twist your right side backward as much as you can. Then lean your head to the right as much as you can. This is how I sit in my wheelchair. Hold perfectly still this way. Then move the thumb and index fingers of both hands. This is what I control. Blink. Move your eyes around without moving your head. What can you see? Now say a few words out loud because you can talk. You can say anything. You can smile. You can frown. You can even sing, if you like. But except for your fingers and your face, you can't move. As you sit there, imagine going to school like this; unmoving in a wheelchair with an attendant. Imagine going to a party, and meeting new people, or going out to dinner. Imagine people staring at you. Imagine meeting someone for the first time.

The point of this is not to get you to feel sorry for me. The point is that I have the same goals and ambitions as you; I just can't reach them in the same way. My brain and my wits and my personality are intact just like yours. My emotions and desires are the same as yours. My intelligence, my hopes and dreams are the same as yours. My good and my bad, my instincts, my joy and my sorrow, my selfishness and my generosity, my despair and my faith are all the same as any young man's. I just can't move like you. I am you, trapped in an unresponsive body.

Chapter 1

TODAY

My Brothers Nathan & Alex

I was born with congenital merosin-deficient muscular dystrophy. It is a rare and recently-recognized type of muscular dystrophy; virtually unknown as of 30 years ago. Muscular dystrophy, or MD as most people call it, is a genetic disease of the muscles. Your body can't synthesize essential proteins, so your muscles just don't grow properly. There are more than 30 kinds of MD; the most common is Duchene's.

Because of MD, I can't stand, walk, lift my arms, feed myself, dress myself, bathe myself, drive a car, or do the many other things everybody else takes for granted. For a while, I believed my life was worthless. That was before I realized how much a person can do if he is willing to find a way.

I've had more than one near-death experience, but I'm a survivor. I've survived physically, but I had to learn to survive mentally and emotionally as well. That's what this story is about. There were many times I wanted to give up and die. I thought about suicide. For years, I was so bitter, angry and unpleasant. It was hard to be around me. But now, every day that I wake up is not only a blessing, but also an opportunity. I have learned to not worry about where I will be 20 years from now, because the truth is, I could die tomorrow. Every day, I strive to do, to love and to appreciate everyone and everything in my life.

When I was a baby, I looked completely normal. I was adorable but I was a physically weak and lethargic baby. Nobody, least of all my parents, knew there was anything seriously wrong with me. It takes a while for MD to show itself.

In fact, the most common type of MD, Duchene's, often doesn't show itself until kids are about four or five years old. At about four or five years old, they start to trip and have problems with their legs. Imagine the dismay of parents discovering their perfectly "normal" child has this deadly congenital disease! Many people with MD die young. With Duchene's, it's anywhere from 18 to 25 years old, although new kinds of care and research are extending life for many young adults with Duchene's MD. Some are now able to have families and live into their 40s.

My prognosis is different. I never crawled or walked, but I may live longer than the average MD patient. Due to the rarity of my MD, there isn't any way of knowing for sure. There's no track record. Duchene's keeps getting worse and worse until it kills you. We now know that Merosin-deficient muscular dystrophy progresses to a certain point and then stops. I think of it like this: Merosin-deficient muscular dystrophy just kind of chews you up, spits you out and then says,"OK, I'm done. Let's see what you can do with that!" As of today, I am 28 years old and still going strong.

Although I'm in a wheelchair, I am not paralyzed. I can move all my body parts, but no more than a wiggle. Since birth, I have had torticollis, which is a muscle tightening in my neck that makes my head lean sideways. I used to be able to turn my head left, right, forward and backwards – though not too far backward. If I leaned my head too far back, I would become unbalanced and fall over. I can't turn my head in any direction any more because of contractures.

Contractures (tightening of connective tissue and muscle in the limbs and joints) are a typical result of having muscular dystrophy. Picture contractures as ever-tightening steel cables inside of you. They pull parts of your body into a non comfortable torque and immobilize them. I have contractures in my neck, knees, elbows, wrists, spine and hips. You name a spot, I've got a contracture. Because of contractures and scoliosis (curvature of the spine), my rib cage has twisted backward on my right side. My lung on that side is so compressed it's pretty much useless. My head is twisted back over my right shoulder. My hands are pulled back toward my upper arms. My legs and ankles are not so contracted but they're very skinny. They are weaker than my upper body because I have never been able to walk. I used to be able to lift my arms and legs. Today, somebody has to lift my arm so I can scratch my nose. If a mosquito lands on my leg, I have to let it bite me until somebody else smacks it.

My brother Alex before his 5K race

Due to contractures, I've lost most of my mobility. Before the age of 12, I could pick up a few pounds. I could use the computer, play chess, do puzzles, play the piano and even feed myself. Not anymore; my wrists are too contracted and my arms are too weak. I can still play video games and use my cell phone, though. Someone needs to put the phone or game controller in my hand and position it correctly. Once it's in my hands, I can use my thumbs. They have stayed strong because I use them a lot. With my hands, I can move and direct my wheelchair, too.

I've fought to maintain mobility my whole life. However, when I was younger, the technology wasn't as advanced as it is now. My 16 year old friend, Gavin, who also has Merosin's MD, has kept much more of his mobility. His family had much more medical support than we did when he was diagnosed. He has a wheelchair that can be adjusted so that he can partially stand to stretch out the contractures in his hips. But it's difficult going. It really hurts, and the fight never ends.

I can go just about anywhere in my motorized wheelchair, but there is very little I do for myself. Whoever is taking care of me has to dress me, take me to the bathroom, brush my teeth, feed me, put me to bed and everything in between.

Eating is one of the positive things in my life. I love to eat. I can still eat and chew my food, but because of the contractures, my teeth are not able to touch when I close my mouth. I chew in the back right area of my mouth where the gums are, so when I eat anything with a crunch, it hurts. No nuts!

13

My brothers Nathan & Alex

Internally, I'm as healthy as a horse. I'm not allergic to anything, I've gotten only two colds in eight years, and I've only had the flu once in my life. I believe my body compensates internally for the weakness of my muscles. Gavin, the friend I mentioned who has Merosin's MD like me, never gets sick either.

Sometimes I ache all over. Especially when the air is below 80 degrees F. My muscles are already very tight and contracted, which makes them ache. The cold air makes them cramp even more. If it's very cold out and there is just a breeze, I will begin to cramp. To me pain is my norm; I feel weird if I'm comfortable. I always hurt but I don't really notice it anymore. I only recognize it when there's extra pain.

Today, I live in Florida with my parents. We used to move around a lot because my father is in the military. I grew up in South Carolina, then North Carolina, then Tennessee. I have an older brother, Alex and a younger brother, Nathan. MD is often caused by genes that are passed down from parents, but doctors say that my MD was not that kind. It was a spontaneous genetic anomaly. Nobody else in my family has ever had it.

So many people have helped me learn how to be a better person, to be happy and kind and to embrace every opportunity that comes my way. This is the story of how that happened. I hope my story will help the able, as well as the disabled.

Chapter 2

DIAGNOSIS

Monkey Face

W
e weren't expecting anything to go wrong," says my mom Melisa Hartsell. She's sitting on the small couch next to my dad James Scott Hartsell. They've been married for 34 years.

My mom's face is warm and vivacious. Most people say that she does not age. Her hairstyle is the only thing that changes. Right now, she has blonde, shoulder-length hair. At 50, she looks much the same as she did when she was 23 (the year I was born). She is trim, strong, with penetrating blue eyes that brook no nonsense.

My dad's a fit man with salt-and-pepper hair, cut military style, and wears metal-rimmed glasses. He's every bit a military man. He's a two-star Major General in the U.S. Marine Corps Reserves.

We live in a gated community of similar stucco and terra cotta homes, with well-kept lawns in central Florida. Our house has several bedrooms plus a master bedroom, a spacious eat-in kitchen and a screened back porch. There is an outdoor grill and a swimming pool with a fountain and hot tub. It's a comfortable, lovely nice house they've worked very hard to acquire. It isn't terribly private, though. My mom says there are always people coming and going. It's not some place that she can ever really relax with all of the drama and interactions between me and my nurses. Though the house isn't huge, it gives the impression of spaciousness with lofty ceilings, hardwood floors and sweeping crown molding. There are lots of light, no steps and it's all on one level. I have two small bedrooms separated by a bathroom for myself and my nursing staff. One room is my bedroom, which has my bed and medical equipment. The other room is my man cave. It is filled with a big screen TV, video and gaming equipment, two adjustable tables, bookshelves with my trophies, Marvel artwork everywhere and a big recliner for the 24-hour nurses.

I asked my mom about my birth and she says she had a perfectly normal pregnancy, with both me and my older brother Alex. No one in either my mom or dad's families have ever had any genetic type of health problems or major physical disabilities. Everybody in my family has been healthy at birth. As I talk to her, Mom leans back on the soft fabric of the couch, her eyes staring up to the left at nothing. Behind her, and all around the room, are photographs of the family – one of her three handsome boys with our parents; another of my older brother Alex with his wife and children.

I sit quietly in my wheelchair with my mother's big office to the side, the formal dining room behind me. Mostly, we eat in the kitchen where the ramp emerges off the long hallway that passes the laundry room and exits into the garage. Every once in a while, I will adjust my wheelchair back and forth or from side to side, as somebody else might shift in an armchair while listening. I like to talk. It's a serious effort of self-control for me to let others tell a story.

Here's what my Mom and Dad had to say about my birth and initial diagnosis…

"When Evin was born he was lethargic. He scored low on the APGAR scale. But there didn't seem to be anything particularly wrong." The APGAR scale is a simple evaluation tool doctors use to measure every newborn's health. It rates appearance, pulse, grimace, activity, and respiration. "The birth had been difficult. Evin's shoulder got lodged under my pelvic bone. The nurse had to push on my stomach as I bore down. I was relieved though, because it was the shortest labor of my three deliveries – only eight hours."

"Evin was my only child born in a military hospital. With my two other sons, I chose to give birth in a more natural and home like environment. However, the circumstances at the time of my pregnancy with Evin did not allow for the

My First Haircut

more natural birth I'd hoped to have. A military hospital was a more sterile medical environment, which I did not care for, because Evin was born with a medical condition called torticollis. His torticollis caused his neck muscle to be contracted and his head tilted to one side, which caused his shoulder to get hung up in my pelvis as he was being delivered. Physical therapy for the torticollis was started right away and then PT never stopped. He went two or three times a week starting at two weeks old."

"We knew Evin was physically weak, but we weren't really worried because he seemed a healthy and happy little baby. At birth the doctors knew he had torticollis, but no idea anything else was wrong. As weeks turned into months Evin wasn't reaching the normal milestones for a baby his age. He really had to work just to get into a sitting position. He wasn't trying to turn over or trying to crawl, and it would be months before doctors would be able to determine what we were facing. We thought that eventually Evin would start crawling and walking. The doctors and therapists kept working with him so he would get strong enough to sit up, turn over and crawl."

"When Evin was born on August 3, 1989, we were living in Beaufort, South Carolina, next to the Parris Island Marine Corps military base. Scott was stationed there as a Captain. It was a small community without specialists or resources for a mysterious pediatric illness."

Dad relates…

"Evin was about three months old when we took him to a hospital in Savannah, Georgia and some other area hospitals to have tests done. We didn't know why he wasn't progressing physically… because mentally, he obviously was. For

17

several months, we were seeing doctor after doctor and it was very emotionally draining, it really was, especially for Melisa. First, they did brain scans to rule out tumors or other neurological diseases. When Evin was about six months old, just before leaving South Carolina, we drove several hours to Ft. Gordon, Georgia, to an Army hospital, to do a special EMG test on Evin's muscles. An EMG, or electromyography test, measures the muscle's response to stimulation. It involves sticking needles into the muscles and stimulating them with electrical impulses."

"It was like torture. They had these very long thin needles. They had to get one into Evin's arm and one into his leg and they kept sticking him. The doctors were having a hard time finding his muscle. We knew he had muscles because he could lift his arms then, but at that point in time we didn't know he had only about 20 percent muscle. Evin was screaming and Melisa was bawling. Even the nurses were crying. Emotionally, it was too much for Melisa, but I said, "We've got to get this done. We've got to know the results." But honestly, it was torture for us and Evin."

"Evin was just a baby and he was crying so hard and Melisa just couldn't take it. I said to her, 'You need to leave.' You need to sit in another room where you can't hear Evin crying while they are doing this test". So I had her leave and I held Evin in my arms. I remember thinking that I didn't want our baby son to think we've abandoned him, so I picked Evin up and cradled him in my arms and looked him in the eyes. I kept talking to him while they were performing the procedure. I kept repeating to Evin that I know it hurts but we have to do it to try to help you."

"Evin couldn't understand; his eyes were so big. He was basically saying, "Dad, save me! Save me!" But we had to finish the test. Eventually, they were able to find some muscle. And once they got it in his muscle, Evin could hold still for a bit while they got a baseline reading. Then they had to stimulate his muscles by putting a little bit of shocks into the needle to see how his muscles contracted. Well, obviously that hurt. Not heavy shocks, but still a shock. So again, that was torturing us both."

"The whole procedure took about 30 minutes. And the whole time, Melisa was in the other room… understandably emotional. It was just too much for her. When it was done, Evin was smiling and happy, like he'd been saved. When we were driving back, I remember Melisa clearly saying, 'We can't do that again.

We're not going to do a test like that again. I don't care what Evin has. We're not going to put him through that again. Even if it's to know how he is going to end up." And I said okay, but I remember thinking, we just don't really know what other tests and procedures he might have to go through."

Back to Mom...

"It was really a hard and emotionally devastating episode. But later, when those test results finally came back, we were able to take Evin to Bethesda Naval Hospital for his next set of tests and a muscle biopsy."

"When Evin was eight months old, we left Parris Island, S.C. and moved to the military base in Quantico, Virginia. We were stationed so Scott could attend a nine-month Officer's school. While we were there, the doctors admitted Evin to Bethesda Naval Hospital for about three days and did every test imaginable. Scott was away in a nearby state on a training mission when they called with the results. They requested I come in to go over the results in person. So my friend CeCe watched our older son, Alex, and I loaded Evin in the van for the 90 minute drive to the Washington, D.C. hospital."

"I sat in the doctor's office with Evin in the stroller next to me, still not thinking that there was anything seriously wrong. Evin was only 9 months old, and to us, it seemed like he was just slow in his physical development. We had no reason to think differently, because otherwise he was healthy and normal. We were not expecting anything too serious, much less devastating. I remember the small office and that the doctor, who was an older woman, was sitting behind her desk. She began to explain all of the tests performed over the three long days and to go over the results. I was really just waiting for her to say, "This is what Evin has, but here's how we are going to fix it." After what seemed like an eternity, she proceeded to explain that Evin had a neuromuscular disease. I said, "OK, well what do we do to fix that?" It didn't even occur to me that this was a disease he was going to have for the rest of his life! The doctor then explained that Evin might not survive past the age of twelve. He had congenital muscular dystrophy. They had taken a muscle biopsy and found that there was a lot of gristle and fat, but very little muscle."

"I remember gathering my things and Evin and proceeding back out to the van to head home. I honestly can't remember much of what happened after that. I remember getting back in the van with Evin but I was in shock! I had taken

Evin to the doctor so many times before. By nine months old, we'd been to the doctor more times than I cared to think about! I wasn't expecting something so serious and not sure at the time that I truly comprehended just how serious it was. It just didn't sink in. We'd gone day-to-day never knowing why or what was really wrong, but it didn't seem that bad because he was such a happy and cute baby. When I went into the doctor's office, I was thinking, let's just get the diagnosis and then we'll figure out how to fix it."

"I left the doctor's office and I still had no answers. There was no conclusion. There were still only questions. There was no answer as to 'what do we do?' I left with more questions and more uncertainty. I thought, wow, this could be really serious; this is not going away."

"Not until I got into the van... driving home, did it really hit me. I was driving down I-95, and it suddenly hit me like a ton of bricks. I remember it was about 4:00 in the afternoon, and rush hour had just begun as I headed south out of DC. I was driving almost on autopilot as my mind wandered off in thought... As a kid I'd always watched the Jerry Lewis telethon for muscular dystrophy – every year. I loved it, but that's really all I knew about muscular dystrophy. I never thought it would affect me personally. I was thinking about the boys on the telethon and the stories of those who didn't live."

"There was so much traffic! As I thought of Evin and this now uncertain future I could feel the emotion coming up. Tears started to come and I could barely see the road, so I pulled over to the side of the road and burst into tears. I'm not sure how long I sat there crying, but at one point I remember turning around to look at Evin. He was just sitting there staring at me with those big blue eyes and his sweet smile. He was so happy! In that moment, Evin looked so sweet, carefree and angelic. He didn't have a clue.... he was just happy to be cared for and loved."

"For the longest time, I felt extremely guilty, as if it was my fault."

"Evin would emphatically protest that it wasn't his fault."

"I carried Evin; I created Evin so to speak. So I felt guilty. Thoughts were running through my head. What do I do? What will happen? How long will we have Evin? Surely they will find a cure. This is what we hung our hopes on for years. A cure would be found for his disease! For the moment, I knew I just wanted him to be healthy and have a happy life. I just didn't know if that was going to happen. As a mother, you want to fix it. I wanted to take it all away and I couldn't."

Dad explains…

"I was out with the Marines on a four day training exercise when Melisa got *the* diagnosis. Somebody came and told me that our senior Colonel wanted to see me. I thought that I was in trouble. I was about 29 years old, just a Captain at the time. Why would this senior Colonel be looking for me by name?"

"When I went to see him he said, "I want you to come and sit down," and he took me into a private room. Then I thought, Oh, no, I'm really in trouble! He said, "I have to share some news about your family." I immediately thought, 'oh no, what in the world has happened to Melisa?" I thought Melisa had been in a car wreck or something. I didn't know what was going on! The Colonel said, "I just got a call and I spoke to your wife. She said she had taken your son Evin to Bethesda and they had diagnosed him with muscular dystrophy."

"At first, honestly, I felt relieved because I had thought it might have been a car wreck, or that Melisa or one of the boys had been seriously injured. But then I thought, OK, it wasn't that kind of serious. We had known something was wrong with Evin because he wasn't walking or crawling, but he was healthy otherwise. So I thought, OK, muscular dystrophy. Of course I didn't know what that meant, what it entailed or what the future would hold. It was just a name at that point and we had no idea what all that meant."

"Then, the Colonel told me he was sending me home. I remember thinking that we were halfway through our exercise so I said, 'Thank you, sir, but I think it'll be okay if I stay for the remaining 2 days. I remember thinking that Evin's health was okay and this was just a diagnosis. He wasn't going in the hospital or having surgery. But the Colonel said, "No I'm sending you home so you can be with your wife because she needs you right now." And of course he was right. I'm so glad that the Colonel had that kind of life experience and wisdom because as soon as he said it I really did want to be there with Melisa. I was thinking about how the news must be affecting her."

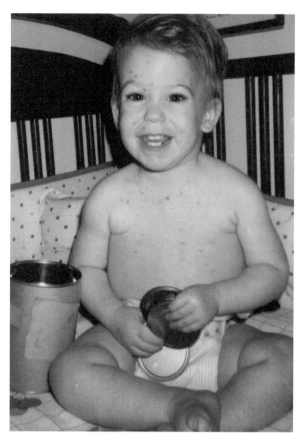

Me with Chickenpox

Chapter 3

MOBILITY

When I was young, about three years old, I didn't even know I was disabled. Everything was new. Everything was interesting. Life for me was like it is for most little kids. Exciting! Until about the age of 12 or 13, I didn't think about what was wrong with my life. I had no bitterness or even sadness. Certainly, I didn't struggle with depression or suicidal thoughts. I was happy.

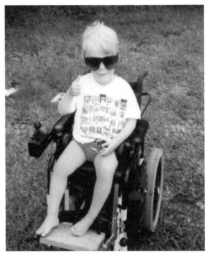

First Wheelchair (Age 3)

I couldn't crawl or walk, but that didn't bother me. I didn't know I was supposed to be crawling and standing by the age of two. I did, however, find my own mode of transportation. At this time, we lived in a small one-story house in Beaufort, South Carolina. There was a small front yard with a sandbox and a swing hanging from a tree, but my mobility was limited outside. Mostly, Mom would hold me on her lap on the swing in the front yard. Inside the house, however, I could go anywhere by scooting on the floor. My arms weren't strong enough to lean on and my legs weren't strong enough to pull me forward, so in order to scoot, I would lean from side to side with my legs straight out in front of me, moving like a penguin on my butt. To go around corners, I'd bend my knees and let them fall to one side, which would rotate my pelvis, then start scooting in a new direction. Since we had no stairs in the house, just about every place was accessible to me.

Being on the ground, scooting around, I couldn't reach to get anything higher than my face, which was only about two feet off the ground. So at age three I couldn't reach anything on a shelf or a dresser or a table. Somebody would have to pick me up to reach anything over two feet off the ground. I'd get frustrated and whine until somebody came. This worked with my mom, but not so much with my dad. I did get a tiny pop on my hand or hip, just like my brother, if they thought I was getting too entitled.

Dangerous Ride

Scooting was great, but my parents wanted to give me more mobility. So they got me a big-wheeled toy tricycle for indoors. Because I couldn't lift myself up, my parents would have to put me on it. But once they did, look out! I just had to be careful because I would get very excited and I had … and have to this day… a large and very heavy head. If I leaned too far either way, I couldn't hold myself up. I would get that slow motion *Ohh nooo* feeling and before I could say, "Help," I would fall and smack my head on the ground. I never really bled or cried like most youngsters. It turns out I was really hard-headed. *(I still am to this day, only most people call it "stubborn".)* After this happened a few times though, my parents put a padded helmet on me when I rode my tricycle.

My disability wasn't an issue to me because walking is really about going from point A to point B. So scooting or riding around on my tricycle was–at that time–a fine replacement for walking. As long as I could get to the toy or whatever else it was I wanted across the room, I was happy.

My big brother Alex and I played together a lot. He was three years older than me, and he always helped and watched out for me. He would lift me onto my trike when I fell off and run around the house with me. We generally rough-housed like any other brothers. One of our favorite games was bouncing on the bunk beds. Mom or Dad would put me on the upper bed and Alex would lie down on the lower bed. Then he'd push up on the springs of the upper bunk with his feet so I'd go flying in the air. I loved it! Imagine always being earthbound like me and then suddenly flying, weightless! I remember one time shouting at Alex, "Higher! Higher!" Alex pushed harder and harder on the springs and I was flying up to the ceiling, screaming with glee. All of a sudden, Alex saw something hurtling down beside him. I'd gone straight up, over the edge of the bed rail and fell to the floor. Splat!

Alex and Evin Camping

Alex screamed and called for Mom. By the time Mom came in to the room, I was laughing. I told you, I have a really hard head!

Another game we had–this was when we were a little older, living in Memphis – was racing downstairs. Our old house had no stairs, so stairs were new to me and of course, something on which I could play. I couldn't go up the stairs by myself, but I could scoot down the stairs one step at a time. My parents, who wanted me to have as much mobility as possible, taught me how to do this as soon as we moved into the new house.

One time Alex and I had just finished playing a video game and we headed downstairs to play outside as usual. Alex loved to race and told me I couldn't beat him down the stairs. I was excited, not thinking, and I started scoot-racing ahead of Alex down the steps. He got excited and scooted past me. Suddenly, I was behind. I was only about two steps down, trying to go even faster. Without realizing, I leaned too far forward. I got that slow motion,*"Oooooh noooo"* feeling and started to tumble. I fell all the way down the stairs, flying right past Alex, and smashed into the wall at the bottom. Mom came running over. Admittedly I was bruised, but I didn't break anything. And best of all, I won!

I loved having an older brother, and when my younger brother Nathan was born, I was so excited to be an older brother. It was always something I secretly wanted because, up until then, people had always looked out for me. Now I would be able to do the same for somebody else. I now got be someone who looked out for another. Unfortunately, it turned out that Nathan got the short end of the stick because of my disability. Having a little brother usually means that the baby gets most of the attention. But when you have a disability, you still get a lot of attention from your parents and it took that away from Nathan. I needed help doing everything, just like a newborn, even though I was already three. I could do little more than an infant for myself.

The attention didn't just stop at my physical needs. My parents seemed to give me more emotional attention, too. Doctors told my parents that my life span would be shorter than either of my brothers. They just didn't know how long I'd be around. Getting all this attention was fun in the moment. I learned that if I whined and cried the right way at the right time, I could get whatever I wanted. But looking back, getting more than my fair share eventually created a rift between Nathan and me. It was bad for Nathan and it was bad for me. For me, it led down a road of entitlement and rudeness.

I didn't look much different from the average three-year-old. I was the same size proportion-wise; at that time, I had no contractures yet, and I used the same body language. Except for weak muscles, I was really pretty much the same as every body else. Then I got my wheelchair. We all go through trials and tribulations in life. Overcoming these obstacles are milestones; they are key to our progress through life. But when you are disabled, you miss a lot of these common experiences – the frustrations and falls as well as the accomplishments. For disabled people though, there are different milestones. The milestones that are unique milestones that others may never get to experience.

My first real milestone, at the age of three, wasn't walking or getting my own clothes on or learning to use the bathroom. It was getting my very first motorized wheelchair. Until that moment, I had always had people following me around, being my arms and legs and even my eyes. I had a hard time seeing my surroundings. This was not because my eyes were bad, but because I couldn't turn my head due to my neck muscles being so tight and weak. If I wanted to see something behind me, somebody had to turn me around. I could turn around myself, but it would take much longer and it was tiring.

But when I got my first wheelchair, I knew what it meant to be free. It was smaller than your average chair. Also, it was around 150-pounds with a light green coat of paint over the metal. It had a light brown wooden footrest with a metal pipe on either side and a joystick on the right side that controlled the chair. Now I had always been a dare devil, but add a 150-pound chair and I truly became a force to be reckoned with! It may surprise you to know where a wheelchair can go. I drove it through snow, thick grass and mud and once, even tried to drive through a pond ... a small pond. That didn't work out too well. My parents and every other adult would shout, "Slowdown, Evin,"because no matter where I went–the mall,church, or my neighborhood – I was always going at top speed: five miles an hour. As I mentioned, I was already hard-headed and wouldn't listen.

With my new chair, I was finally able to determine where I went without assistance. It was the first time I experienced the freedom of mobility. People would say, "Evin, you drive your wheelchair better than I drive my car." I thought it was funny because how can a three-year-old be better at driving. I felt like nothing could stop me, whether it be a door or someone's feet. Like many three-year olds, I pushed my limits. I truly believe I was not supposed to walk, because I was born to drive a wheelchair.

My mom sent my dad a picture of me in the wheelchair. He was on a 6-month deployment over seas at the time. In the picture, I was perilously close to his brand-new black truck and he was scared I'd hit it. But Mom sent him a video, too. He always said he was amazed by it, and just like Mom was so amazed at the mobility and the movement control I had. We talked about it recently and here's what he said, word for word (I recorded him): *"Son, I can tell you, me watching you with that smile on your face, and you having your own mobility for the first time, going where you wanted to go without somebody carrying you or pushing you; you playing in that wheelchair, it was one of the brightest times in my life. Especially when I was missing everybody so much while being on deployment, and that was such a positive thing. I watched it over and over again, cause that smile on your beautiful face was amazing. You were playing with a soccer ball and engaging. You were taking the ball from your older brother Alex and hiding it under your chair so he couldn't get to it. So you were pissing him off, but that was your control and you were loving it and smiling the whole time. It was just very, very encouraging to watch you, how fast you could go. It was amazing, as a three-year old, you had such control and mobility and dexterity backing up, turning. Everybody I proudly showed it to, was amazed. It changed your personality. It was so positive and so encouraging."*

At first, kids in the neighborhood were a little afraid. They wondered … should I go over and talk to that kid or avoid him? They wanted to run from me out of fear, but not judgment. At the same time, they were curious. My older brother Alex helped the other children to see that I was just like one of them. Alex didn't see me as different. All he had ever seen was me, adjusting to my disability. He was surprised at times when the other kids were uncomfortable with me, but it all worked out well. The moment the other kids found out they could use me as a jungle gym and get free rides or have me sling-shot them with their roller blades, they seemed to completely forget I was a scary new thing. I became a friend.

I played soccer with my wheelchair, too. I'd use my chair to hit the ball. I could trap it under the plate and sort of dribble it forward. When I stopped, the ball would be released, unless it got trapped under the chair. Sometimes the ball would flip the chair over and slam my face into the ground. Thanks to my giant head, I didn't get any bruises or scratches. Somebody would help me get up, and we'd go on playing.

At the time, the wheelchair made me not only understand my differences, but it also helped me lessen my differences. It helped me become able. Up until then, I never thought I was a disabled kid. But now, it hit me in a big way, that wow, I am different. I didn't really know how or why, and I didn't really care. I just knew I was different. The great thing about being disabled from birth is that you don't know what you're missing because you never had it from the start. For me, ignorance truly was bliss.

Alex and I continued to push the limits, horsing around. We liked to experiment to see what the wheelchair could do. One time Alex tied a rope around a tree and the other end to my wheelchair. Then I drove as fast as I could around and around the tree. As the rope pulled tight and I revved forward, suddenly the wheelchair was yanked completely off the ground into the air. I landed, still strapped into the wheelchair, on my side. Alex finally had to cut the rope to get me free.

In winter, I loved driving the chair fast and slamming on the brakes, which allowed me to skid on the ice and snow. This was especially effective when skidding around the corner into the street. Fortunately, we didn't ever cause a traffic accident or get run over. I also loved it when my dad put soapy water on the smooth garage floor, and I'd race in sliding and skidding having fun. I got so excited one time, I went too fast and smacked a hole in the back of the garage wall. Dad stopped soaping the floor after that. Popping a wheelie, aka the "Bronking Bull," was another favorite trick. The back of the chair was so heavy, I'd turn up the speed, go from zero to top speed, or just go back and forward really fast. The front wheels would come off the ground. But my most favorite thing to do to this day with my wheelchairs is to spin around in circles. I could spin around in circles all day and never get nauseous.

At the age of 28, I wish I could go back to that place where you don't care about your disability, about discrimination or being judged. Children accept other people at this age for who they are and not what they are. The other kids didn't judge me, and they didn't discriminate against me. After all, the world was new from their point of view as well. The kids on my block had never been educated about disability or even seen a wheelchair before. For us, the wheelchair was awesome; it was a giant toy that gave me the mobility I'd never had before.

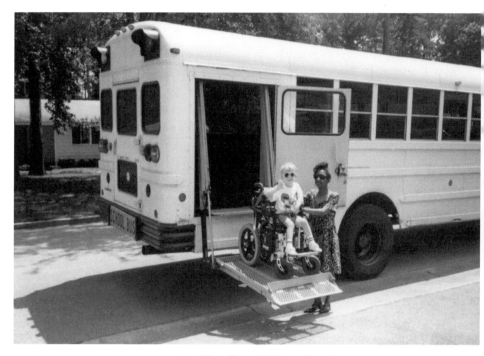

My Chauffeured Ride to PreK

Chapter 4

IT WAS NOT TOO MUCH FOR ME

Mom just returned home from her job as a real estate broker. She looks tired and hot. She pulls her hair back into a ponytail, takes a bottle of water from the fridge and leans against the counter. *She says*, "A lot of my family thought it was crazy to have another child. Your brother, Nathan, was born when you were three. Muscular dystrophy doesn't run in the family so I thought nothing of it. The doctor said it was a fluke; a gene mutation. If it was inherited, it would have come from one of our families but there was no one we knew of in our families, who had a neuro muscular disease. The odds were slim to none for having another child to be born with this disease."

A Mother's Love

"Maybe I missed the milestones with you, sitting up, walking … I don't know. Everybody thought I was crazy, but I wanted another child. Even your Dad wondered if we should have another baby with you only being two. He even tried to talk me out of it. We both knew you were going to be a lot of work. Or did we? I'm not sure we comprehended what the future could bring. To be honest I believed a cure was just around the corner. I believed you would be cured of this disease and walk some day. I wanted to believe it so desperately! I knew your Dad was going to be gone on military duty often, but I wanted another baby. I didn't give much thought to the extra work because then again I hoped for a cure and had faith there would be one some day. After Nathan though, I decided to have my tubes tied. Nathan was healthy and I was thankful. "It's permanent," said the doctor. I was only 27 at the time. I had three kids; one with a disability. I said, "Cut them!" I didn't want any accidents. I haven't given it a second thought or regretted it."

"Oh my goodness, it was so hard. In many ways, it was like having two newborns. You were three and to some extent, you could do things yourself, but I had to dress and feed you both. I couldn't leave you alone in the bathtub. It was harder than having twins because as babies grow up, they get stronger and more independent. But it was getting harder and harder to take care of you. As you grew, you were getting weaker instead of stronger. You got heavier and was harder to lift. Emotionally, it was difficult too. It hurt my heart to watch you grow up and watch you struggle with the simplest tasks of playing with a toy or the pain of physical therapy every week. As you got older, your peers would exclude you from activities. It hurt me to see how it affected you emotionally as you struggled with the feeling of just wanting to belong. I thought about how you would never become independent. It was always going to be this hard. You would never be able to do things on your own. It was so overwhelming. Especially if you or your brothers were sick and your dad was gone. I'd be up all night, no sleep, no breaks." After several days of it, I'd be deeply exhausted.

Once, Alex said to me, 'Mom, I never saw you cry!' I replied, "Oh, I cried. I went in the closet and cried."

"When your dad was home he would help however he could. Both with the boys and with the stress. But since he was a Marine Officer, he was pulled away often to get his unit ready for deployment. My family was far away; and then your dad had to go away; deployed over seas to Iraq and then later to Afghanistan. I had to do it all when he was away. I felt I couldn't show any weakness. Now, looking back, I think it was a disservice to my kids to not show how I felt; how I struggled at times. 'Mom's taking care of it all. Mom's so strong!' (I heard this from others as well as telling myself) I am strong! But those around me didn't see I was just surviving. I was good at wearing a mask of strength, putting up somewhat of a force field around me."

"Survival: That's the word that comes to mind. I put on a good face. I was stubborn, I never wanted to admit it was too much for me, or even that I needed help. I really did need help but didn't know how to ask. I believe this

New Baby Brother

32

must have started, – this mind-set,–it must have started when I got married so young! I was only sixteen."

"I remember going out with the other military wives shortly after her marriage, when I joined your Dad who was 21 and posted at the school for new Marine officers at Quantico, Virginia. They were all in their 20's, and here I was sixteen years old. I just faked it. I didn't know what I was doing. Needless to say, I didn't feel comfortable enough to develop real friends among the other wives. I didn't want to show any uncertainty or seem childish to them. But to tell you the truth, I was still a child. I was still a child, and I lost my childhood. I believe it was then that I started creating this mask of adulthood to not be embarrassed of the things I didn't know or experiences I had not had. I was very shy and introverted so it was difficult for me to make friends or even go out in public. I spent a lot of time alone during those early years of marriage."

"There were years of resentment and rage toward my parents, toward my mom and dad, for persuading me to marry at such a young age. "Your Dad was my boyfriend, and he was 5 years older. I don't know what my parents were thinking! I was only sixteen. I wasn't even finished with high school. Maybe they were afraid I'd get pregnant. I felt like they stood on the sidelines and allowed me to make this adult decision, and they basically gave my childhood away."

"I was stubborn and at first, I wanted to get married. But on the day of my wedding, we went for the obligatory interview with your Dad's military commander. The commander said we shouldn't do it, That we should wait because I was too young. He explained what it's like for a military wife; how much I was going to be alone, how much I'd have to do on my own and how I'd have no family around because we'd always be moving. It scared me." After the interview with the commander, I tried to tell your Dad I thought perhaps we should wait, but he didn't agree. Your Dad knew I was young, but he felt that I really acted and seemed so mature, and he loved me and felt that he could really make me happy and take care of me for the rest of our lives. When they got back home, I told my parents that I did not want to go through with the marriage. But they insisted. "They said it was already decided. It was already planned and I had to go through with it. I was told it was just my nerves and that I really wanted to get married."

"So I did. The plan was that I would keep living at home in Pensacola,

Florida and finish high school while your Dad went back to the military training base in Virginia. But something had changed in me. I didn't want my parents telling me what to do any more. I was a married woman now, and I didn't think they should be giving me a curfew." After just a month, I left home and went to join your Dad on the base in Quantico, Virginia. At least we knew enough not to have children right away. I was 19 when Alex was born; 22 when you were born; and 25 when Nathan was born. Reality was that due to your Dad's military duties I was on my own with the kids much of the time."

"Not long after Nathan was born, your dad went out on a six-month military overseas deployment. When you boys were little, I believe I went through periods of depression and there are lapses in my memories. I think maybe I struggled with postpartum depression, especially after your birth, Evin. Your dad would work six days a week during the six months leading up to a deployment and then be gone for 6 months overseas on the deployment. If you or your brothers were sick, I was up all night with you and then up all day."

"Your dad was worried about us when he was gone, but I couldn't talk to him about what was going on back home. He wanted me to talk about it, but I just didn't want to worry him. I felt that the stress he was dealing with getting his Marines ready for war was enough! I thought I'd just handle it and tell him when he returned."

"For example, when Nathan was about seven or eight months old and you were almost four, we were in a car accident. Your dad was very close to finishing his 6-month deployment and he would be home in just two weeks. I'd just spoken with him on the Saturday before his ship departed from Spain returning to the U.S. and we wouldn't be able to talk again until he arrived home. On Sunday we were in the van going to a fair. I looked both ways and pulled out into an intersection, but a low tree branch was blocking my view. A car smashed right into the van, T-boning us. You were up front with me in a car seat with your wheelchair strapped down in the back. I remember the shock of the accident and calling 911. You were hurt in that accident from the impact. It turned out that the femur in your right leg was broken. The doctors put you in a cast from your hip down to your foot and then put a half-cast on your left leg with a bar across to the right leg so you couldn't move your legs at all. You couldn't even sit up. We'd been in the hospital a day or two when I told the doctors that I thought this wasn't a good idea. I explained to them that you had a muscle disease and that being cast this way could do more damage to you and weaken the muscles in your legs even further."

"However, no one was listening to my concerns and they weren't offering up a solution to the problem that I expressed. I guess the doctors thought I didn't know what I was talking about and continued on with their protocols. Your dad was on a ship and I couldn't talk to him about it, so I had to make this decision on my own. It seemed like the doctors didn't understand the seriousness of your condition; they were focused on the fracture, not your muscle condition. I was so frustrated, I ended up checking you out of the hospital and literally carrying you out of the hospital in my arms. I called a friend to pick us up in her van and she took us home. I remember my friend saying, 'You are crazy for leaving the hospital!' but I knew I was doing what was best for you."

"The only way I could contact your dad was for me to send him a Red Cross emergency message. But I didn't want to worry him, and I didn't think there was anything he could do until he got home anyway. I agonized over the decision for days but I didn't send it. I felt there was nothing he could do aboard a ship except worry. There was no sense in putting him through that stress."

"After we got home from the local military hospital I started making phone calls. I found a doctor at Duke University who specialized in orthopedics but also understood neuromuscular diseases. When I explained to him the situation he said, "Oh my God, get him up here immediately." The doctor took you right into surgery and put a steel plate and screws in your right leg to fix the fractured femur bone. My mother came up from Florida immediately to help with Alex and Nathan until you dad returned from his deployment."

"When your dad came home two weeks later, I gave him a big hug and immediately said, 'We need to talk before we head home.' He took me in an office so we could have a private conversation. First, he was shocked to find out that his mother-in-law was there after he had been gone for 6-months and he was further shocked to find all that had happened in the two weeks since our last conversation. I told him about everything after it was all over, of course. That happened a lot during those early years before there was email and cell phones. We had this running joke in the family that every time Scott left town something major was going to happen. This seemed to be the case in the years to come, but only it wasn't so funny."

"As I began to meet other families who had children with MD, I saw how they were devastated by this disease! The stress level in many cases was just too much for families to handle. We grew closer to these families dealing with MD and saw the destruction of the disease, both physical and emotional. It took a toll on the families, the siblings, and the grandparents. It was what I like to call a domino effect. Whoever came into contact with this disease, it adversely affected. Our family was no exception. The strain of your dad's military career and frequent absence, combined with your disability created overwhelming stressors on our marriage." I credit our commitment to our faith, as well as each other for holding us together during this time."

"Your disease was hard on both Alex and Nathan. It was harder for Nathan to understand because of his being the baby of the family. He didn't understand the extra attention you received. I really made it a point to make sure Nathan and Alex got what they needed but I was stretched so thin all of the time and I didn't have help until you were 18. I know I failed many times in meeting you and your brothers needs but I tried. At 18, you qualified as an adult with a disability which meant you would be eligible for nursing care through Medicaid. Until a child is 18, in most cases, all the in-home-care for a disabled child has to be handled by the parents or family members."

"I was visiting my grandmother in Alabama and my aunt probably saw me going through everything I had to do to take care of Evin and the boys, everything it entailed, and I had no nursing help. She said this was all too much for me; I should put you in a home where somebody else could take care of you. It infuriated me! I said to her: Let me put you in a home when you get old and let someone else take care of you instead of your family! It didn't matter what the issues were, I was determined to persevere."

Not taking care of you was never an option! I redoubled my efforts at helping you to grow strong, even while I was assailed with doubt and fear. Nobody could give us a real prognosis. "We worked on your strength in physical therapy and at home. They wanted to strengthen your core,your stomach and back, to give you more strength for the long run. I would look at you when they were working with you and think: Are you even going to be around when you're 12? The uncertainty of your future was just so difficult to face."

"When you were little, you looked just like every other child. You couldn't tell there was anything wrong. You'd sit on the floor playing with toys, and the other kids would sit on the floor and play with toys, too. You didn't see many different. Except, I carried you everywhere! After Nathan was born, I'd carry him in a carry all and you on my hip. We would go grocery shopping, I'd have Nathan in the carry all and you would sit in the shopping cart. When your dad could go with us to the grocery store he'd always make a game out of burying you under the groceries in the shopping cart and you Boys loved it. You loved both the attention and the food piled up around you like a fort. Nobody noticed there was anything wrong with you."

"Around that time, you started getting some of the contractures you have now. Your muscles and tendons were tightening up. When you were about three, your elbows started tightening up. We had these inflatable arm bands like long water-wings that I had to put your arms in to at night. They went from your biceps to your wrists. They were supposed to help prevent the contractures or keep them from getting worse. You hated it! They were hot and sweaty at night and you didn't understand what they were for. I wasn't even sure if they really made a difference but we felt we had to try something."

"Not long after that, we got a machine called a Prone Stander that you had to be strapped to in order to stand you up and help stretch out your hips and knees and ankle contractures. There was a tray in the front of it so you could play while you stood. Alex would bring you toys to try and take your mind off the pain. It was intended to be used to stretch out your hips and to put weight on your legs and feet. Every time we put you in it you would cry and we couldn't tell if it really was hurting you or if you just weren't used to being in that standing upright position."

~ Both my Mom and Dad hated it. They had to put me in it a couple of times a week and it really bothered them seeing me cry every time I was in it. To me, the stander was a torture machine. I can still remember it. Mom would lay me down flat on a cold, hard surface and strap me in tightly – chest, hips, knees, ankles. Then she would tilt the whole thing up. For me, just the anticipation was frightening. The pain was terrible, but so was the fear. The straps across my chest made me feel like I couldn't breathe. I had never experienced pain like that before.

I would cry the whole time and wonder why my mom and dad were doing this to me. There were ankle braces, too. They were made out of form-fitting plastic as hard as steel with sharp edges that extended from just shy of my toes up to just above the ankle. The ankle braces had to be worn at night or sometimes inside my shoes. They hurt. They hurt, they were sweaty and they caused sores on my skin.

Another device that was supposed to correct the torticollis was a plastic helmet-shoulder-pad combination that pushed down on my left shoulder in an effort to push my head back up straight. It gave me headaches and rubbed my hair off where it touched. Instead of pushing my head up, my shoulder was getting pushed down. So thankfully my parents discontinued using that device!

When I was almost six years old, dad left Active Duty and transitioned to the Reserves and he got a civilian job in Memphis, Tennessee where his mother lived. I was not covered by health insurance for a year because I had a pre-existing condition. Mom believes that during that one-year hiatus, when I could not get physical therapy, my contractures worsened considerably.

The only other person I know that has the same type of Merosin's MD that I have is Gavin Grubbs. Today Gavin is 16 years old and has less severe contractures and much more mobility than I did at that age. Gavin's mother, Mindy Grubbs, attributes this to their ability to live and stay in one place where they had wonderful doctors, a great support system, and continuity of care.

The Grubbs Family

"We were blessed with an amazing physical therapist since Gavin was three months old," says Mindy Grubbs. " I think he's been not only a therapist, but an advocate. Not being a military family like the Hartsells, we could stay; we were able to connect with doctors."

Gavin, who also suffers from Merosin's MD, was part of a five-year study at the National Institutes of Health. Beginning when Gavin was about six years old, they would go to Maryland one week each summer. There, the doctors gathered data: mental, physical, emotional … and the Grubbs were able to connect with doctors who were particularly interested in congenital MD like Carson Bonnemann, a doctor Mindy feels was particularly helpful to them.

"Just the ability to talk with each other and doctors," says Mindy, "our Facebook page … we attended a conference this past summer. You get that emotional support, bounce questions off people.

Gavin

"Gavin's elbow is contracted; his hip flexors have contracted; he has a neck contracture – it's not too bad. He looks up. It's a constant battle. It would be better if I stretched him daily for an hour every day, but at some point you have to balance between living and fighting. Do we do everything? Not everything. It's a constant battle."

"We did the stander when Gavin was little. But the therapist worked with us so that he got to be the bad guy instead of me. It wasn't that bad. We just made small adjustments, what he could bear. He had to build up to it. Having the support of this great physical therapist made it less painful.

"Once we were over the puberty hump," says Mindy, "I asked doctor if the contractures would finally stop. And he said, no, we'd always have to fight it." Mindy says she has had a huge support group: close family, close friends. She and her husband live in the small town where they both grew up. She believes that made a big difference for Gavin's development.

My Mom continues, "Alex was such a big help. He was only six when Nathan was born. But he always wanted to help. I'd put you in the walker, you know, with the wheels on it, and I'd be busy doing something with Nathan and Alex would push you all around the house in that wheeled walker. And you would just laugh and laugh." Mom's eyes light up as she laughs thinking of me laughing at that age. "But it was hard. I was alone so much. I could go to the gym. They had a kids' center and they'd watch the kids while I worked out. That was a relief. And I had a friend, Margaret. Sometimes her daughter would babysit and we'd go out to dinner or a movie. But I didn't get a lot of breaks." One of the few breaks I did get was when your Dad would use his travel frequent flyer and hotel stay points to send me and my friend off on a week long get-away vacation usually around Mother's Day, and usually to a beach location in either Florida or Mexico, and one time to Jamaica. Dad would take days off work to be with you Boys while I got a well-deserved and much needed break.

Margaret, a single mother of four, became my closest friend. We met at the gym and she too was struggling. She was holding down a full-time job and raising four kids on her own— I felt we had a lot in common. Knowing how stressed I was, Margaret introduced me to marijuana.

It might have been a set-up for addiction, but I used it medicinally. "I just don't have an addictive personality. I wasn't interested in getting high. I didn't want to escape; I wanted to cope. To me, it was the same as drinking a glass of wine but I didn't like wine at the time."

In particular, marijuana helped me avoid getting angry and taking it out on the kids. "When everything got so crazy I thought I was going to explode, I'd go out in the back yard and take one hit off a joint. Just one hit. I felt the small dose relaxed me enough so I wouldn't lose my temper. "I was always super-responsible. I just wanted to be able to function. Pot gave me more patience and probably prevented a nervous breakdown."

"Much later, after we moved, I no longer had access to marijuana. "I drank a glass of wine at the end of the night sometimes, but like I said, it wasn't often. I didn't want to be impaired. "I'd see other moms make their older children take care of the younger children, and I thought it was wrong. It's a lot of responsibility on older children, and it's not their responsibility!"

"When you were born, Alex was only three, he could get me a diaper but he couldn't do that much, and he shouldn't be doing that much. I didn't want Alex to have to watch the younger kids. It was my responsibility."

"I wanted my children to enjoy their childhood. Children should be allowed to be children. They should not be robbed of their childhood."

"This is a precept I repeated often: The right to a non burdened childhood. It is impossible not to recall my own early marriage, and the incredulity that this could have happened to me: I was only sixteen when thrown into adulthood!"

"I would break down emotionally sometimes, but I didn't want the boys to see me. Because Scott was gone much through the years with both military and civilian work, I felt this responsibility to always show strength and stability to the boys. Evin, you and I were so close, you could immediately pick up on whatever emotion I was feeling and mirror it. I didn't want them to see me like that and become upset as well, so I'd go to the closet to cry. Or scream into a pillow." Whatever gave me the most relief at the time."

Exploring Naval Aviation Museum

Chapter 5

SAVE ME, DAD

Singing church Songs with Dad

Dad sits in his rocking chair, but not at home. He's off working on a key military assignment again. Rocking chairs define Dad's comfort zone. At home, he has one in the living room and another near the kitchen. Mom has the big office space; Dad has his rocking chairs. He's always on the move, even when he's relaxing.

He prefers writing to being interviewed. Or maybe it's just hard to catch up with him. Though he has worked on trying to be at home more, these days he is often away. Like so many of our military, since 9/11, he has been called more frequently from the Marine Reserves to perform periods of active duty in key locations. Just now, he is away on an assignment in the Pacific working as the Director of a Department of Defense Regional Executive Education Center: DKI Asia Pacific Center for Security Studies.

I asked my Dad what was one of the most difficult things you had to deal with from when I was young? *Here is what he said,* "In the fall of 1992 Evin had just turned three years old and we were living in Jacksonville, North Carolina when, I was stationed with the Marines at Camp Lejeune. It was a Wednesday evening and I had just got home from a long hard dirty day at work and Melisa was just about to head out the door to head to our Wednesday evening church services with the three boys. Being as filthy as I was from being out in the field all day, I was unable to make it to church that night so I told Melisa that I would just keep Evin at home with me so she wouldn't have to deal with all three little ones getting in and out of car and getting them all to their Bible classes. She said Evin hadn't eaten his dinner yet and asked me to feed him the hot dog that she made for him."

"I waved to her as she pulled out of the driveway with Alex and Nathan and headed off to Bible classes. Then I took Evin and set him up in the family room in front of the TV, and cut his hot dog up into little half inch size pieces and put them on a little plate, which I set in front of him. He was more interested in the cartoon than eating so I told him "Evin, eat!" And he grabbed a piece and put it in his mouth. I sat there with him for a few moments and watched him pick up a second piece and put it in his mouth and start chewing it. I remember telling him to "be sure and chew it up really good before you put another piece in your mouth" and he said 'Yes Sir,' with a mouth full of hot dogs."

"I told him that I had to go and get a quick shower because I was dirty but that I would come back and check on him when I was done. He looked up and smiled and said, "OK, Daddy," so I headed off to the back of the house to get a shower. I turn on the water letting it get warm and got undressed. As I was doing all this, I asked loudly, "Evin are you OK?" To which he responded "Yes sir." About another 30 seconds went past and the water was finally warm and I was just about to step into the shower, when something in my mind said just check on Evin one more time, so I stuck my head back out of the bathroom and yelled down the hallway, "Evin are you still OK?" I thought I heard a response but it wasn't his usual, "yes sir" this time; it was something that just was different and caught my attention. I hesitated for a moment thinking to myself, I can jump in and jump out of the shower really quick, but whether it was just fatherly instinct, or God's blessed intervention, something made me pause."

"Quickly, I wrapped a towel around myself and walked back down the hall just to check on him one more time. As I walked into the room, I saw Evin sitting there staring straight ahead at the TV but I could tell something just wasn't right. I said, "Evin?" and when I got around in front of him, I saw that his eyes were so wide open, and he was already turning blue, and his little hands and fingers were extended and rigid and were beginning to shake. From my training, I immediately realized he was choking and was not getting air. I grabbed him off the floor, turned him around holding him in front of me with his face away from me, and tried to do something like a Heimlich maneuver with my fist into his stomach trying to help him to cough it up."

"My adrenalin had kicked in and what seemed like minutes was really just seconds. I immediately turned him upside down holding him by his ankles and started jolting him up and down, trying to let gravity and force help dislodge whatever was stuck in his throat. I also reached into his mouth with my finger and could feel a piece of something firm lodged in the back of his throat. He was turning a deeper blue, and the whites of his eyes were starting to turn red. He had a look of pure terror and desperation on his face as he stared at me with his big bulging eyes, clearly communicating with his expression something that was louder than any scream - Daddy help!"

"I realized he was about to die, so with one hand I grabbed both of his ankles continued to jolt him up and down, while I grabbed the telephone with my other hand and dialed 911. Every time I jolted his body, I could hear a little bit of a gurgling sound, so I knew some little bits of air might be getting into him. I spoke rapidly but forcefully to the 911 operator, explaining my situation and she immediately dispatched an ambulance to our house. While I waited for the ambulance to get to our house I continued to shake Evin up-and-down trying help dislodge the obstruction that was preventing air getting into his lungs."

"The ambulance arrived at our house in 12 minutes, even though it seemed like an eternity for me. While the paramedics worked, I threw on some shorts and a t-shirt and grabbed some shoes. From when I first grabbed him off of the floor until I jumped in the ambulance with him, I kept telling Evin, "Daddy's going to save you, I'm going to save you!" The neighbors rushed outside when the ambulance pulled up in front of the house and I yelled to them that Evin was choking and to let Melisa know as soon as she got home from church."

"When we got in the ambulance, the paramedics lay Evin flat on a stretcher and put an oxygen mask on him, but as soon as they did he started turning blue again. The look of terror came back on his face and he reached his little hand toward me silently begging for help again. I told the paramedics that they had to shake him upside down in order to help him get some air but they told me that wasn't the protocol for choking and the oxygen would help. I disagreed but they told me to stay back that they knew what they were doing. I waited about 10 seconds and then moved in and grabbed Evin off of the stretcher and start shaking him upside down as I had before. He started gurgling again. It must have been the look on my face and the command voice that I used when I told the paramedic to "Move" as I grabbed Evin that made them realize that I was in charge and they had better not try to take the child away from his father. As I was jolting Evin, I had them continue to adjust the oxygen mask on his face and we did this in the back of the speeding ambulance all the way to the hospital."

"I ran in with Evin upside down holding him by his ankles and the ER staff looked at me like I was crazy. I laid him on the ER bed and told the Doctor he had something lodged in the back of his throat. As soon as I laid him down he started to turn blue again and the doctor immediately grabbed a pair of long forcep and reached in to the back of his Evin's throat and pulled out a half inch, unchewed piece of hot dog. As soon as the doctor cleared that out of his throat, Evin took in a huge gasp of air and he went from light blue back to his normal color within a matter of seconds right in front of us. Within a matter of another few seconds, Evin looked up at me and said, "I'm sorry Daddy, I tried to chew it." It was at that point that I went where Evin couldn't see me and broke down and sobbed for several minutes."

Poem

Written by

Evin Hartsell

on March 1st 2004

This is a Poem that sounds like a Rap

My Dad's in Iraq and he's busting a Cap

He's a hard charging and motivated Marine

You wouldn't believe all the things he's seen

He rides in a HUMMV in the Desert through Wind and Rain

Get in his way and he'll cause you some Pain

He's travelled all over many Lands and Seas

Protecting the Freedoms of You and Me

He's Camouflaged from head to toe

Where's my Dad?, I don't know

But if you happen to find him before next Year

Tell him I LOVE him and MISS him back here

Save me Dad

Chapter 6

THE MUSCULAR DYSTROPHY ASSOCIATION

I was close to turning six when my father gave up his Active Duty Marine career and transitioned to the Marine Reserves. He had been given the option of moving us all to a new duty station in Okinawa for two to three years, or of going there by himself for just one year. Because of my condition, both Mom and Dad felt that neither of these options were acceptable. Dad wanted all of us all in one place with the best access to the best doctors available.

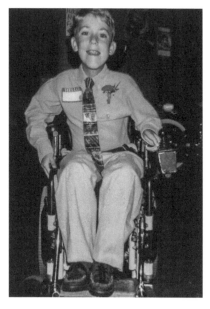

We moved to Memphis, Tennessee where my dad took a civilian job with a medical devices company. This meant we no longer had to move every three years and Dad could be with the family more. My mother and brothers and I would be able to create more long-lasting friendships.

MDA Junior Goodwill Ambassador

Memphis was the first place we lived where we found the Muscular Dystrophy Association (MDA), and it made a huge difference. In Memphis, there was a special clinic just for kids with muscular dystrophy. It was there that my parents met Betty S. and Norma G., who worked at the muscular dystrophy clinic. They were to become very important in our lives. Betty and Norma told my parents about the MDA – an organization that had real information about muscular dystrophy.

Even more important than information, the MDA had a support group, and for the first time, my mom was able to talk to other parents and the volunteers. She says just being around other parents who had children with MD was helpful. But she saw a lot of parents lose their children, and she thought: Eventually that will happen to Evin and us…it will happen one day, we just don't know when…

My mom became a volunteer and did a lot of work with for the MDA. Soon after joining the MDA, Betty told my parents about MDA camp. My mother was less than enthusiastic about me going to camp. She'd never been away from me since I'd been born, with the exception of a few days with my grandparents. She says she spent a lot of time with the other parents and was reassured by them.

My dad says they assumed they'd go with me. Then somebody said to him, "Oh no, you're not going. He will have a counselor with him at camp." And my dad said, "WHAT??!!!" I was going somewhere they'd never seen. Mom was scared. When they took me fishing, what if I fell in? Who's going to be there if I choked? And a whole week … there were no cell phones back then. It was far away and completely unknown. But all the others from the MDA assured my parents that I should go – that I would be fine!

Mom remembers Dad putting me on the bus to camp and thinking, "Oh my gosh, all these people that I don't know are going to be taking care of my boy! A whole week I won't hear from him." She hadn't been away from me for more than an hour! She wanted to get in the car and follow the bus. And everybody around her, they were trying to reassure her: "Mom," they'd say, "we got him…" I didn't see my dad holding my crying mom tightly as I pulled out of the parking lot in the bus.

When I first heard about summer camp, I didn't know what to think. At the age of six, you don't know what camp is except for camping with your dad in the backyard. After my parents explained that the Muscular Dystrophy Association camp was a summer camp for individuals with my type of disability, I began to come around. I was neither scared or worried about being around other disabled people, but it was the first time I would be away from my parents for a week. I was excited and afraid about that.

I had seen other disabled people, but I'd never really interacted with other disabled people before. My main companions were my brothers and neighborhood friends, none of whom were disabled. My brothers and I would often do a lot of the same things together that any siblings do, like playing outside and getting into trouble. But when it came to disabled children, I had no idea what to expect.

As camp-time got closer, though, I realized that this was something no one in my family had ever experienced. This was a place that was designed for

Miss Norma

someone just like me, not them. And for the first time, I would experience true independence from my parents. Most children have a sense of independence when they learn to walk. Even as a toddler, you can run away from your parents if you choose. You can struggle when they pick you up. When they say, "Stop," you can either listen and stop, or you can disobey and keep running. Not me.

You can imagine a child who has never been able to test the waters or push against his parents in a physical way would be aching for a little freedom and independence. Not that I would consider myself all that rebellious, but for me there was an independence that was sorely missing in my life even at this age. That independence wasn't even expressed until this moment when I would leave my parents to go to camp for a week. This was the first time my mother let me go on a trip without her. And when I say "let," I mean it! My mom was very reluctant to let me go. But my father was all for it. After I got on the bus, and my mom was crying, he told her that it was going to be good for me and it would be good for her too.

It was. I would go on to return to MDA camp every summer for the next 11 years. Going to our remarkable camp (brilliantly run by the amazing Norma and a host of dedicated volunteers) was one of the most helpful and formative experiences of my life. And I know that was true for many other children there, as well. Many of us returned year after year. At MDA camp, we finally learned what it meant to be "normal."

Firefighters Fill The Boot

Chapter 7

INDEPENDENCE

MDA Camp

We left the house on a June Sunday morning to get on the bus to camp. Dad carried me on; all of the wheelchairs and equipment went on another bus. He put me down next to my counselor and explained to her how to hold me and make sure I stayed sitting upright as the bus moved along. My dad says it was a little scary ... the counselor looked at him like he was crazy! I arrived safely, though. There were children of all ages on the bus. I was completely oblivious to anybody's physical or mental disability. To all of us, who hadn't yet learned from society to judge others by their race or religion or looks or abilities, we were all just a bunch of kids.

My heart was beating very fast as we rode the bus toward camp because this was my first taste of freedom. One of the first boys I noticed was sitting across from me. Little did I know that he would be a best friend for years to come. Harry R. was a very shy boy who was my own age from Arkansas, from just across the Mississippi River. He was someone of intelligence, and I could tell right away that he was a "book smarts" kind of person. His personality was so different from my own. I was impulsive; I'd rush into things unknown to me. He seemed to be the opposite. He was thoughtful and sometimes fearful, but definitely not impulsive.

The ride from Memphis to camp lasted about three hours. Bikers on their

Harley-Davidsons escorted us and led the bus. They were a group who did fund raisers for us and always accompanied our bus to camp. I watched as the city life of Memphis was slowly replaced by trees of all kinds. The roads shifted from nice paved roads to bumpy side roads and then finally to dirt. I immediately tried to introduce myself but Harry just stared back with quiet reserve. I at least managed to learn his name and that this would be his first trip to camp as well. You might think a three hour bus ride would be hard on anyone's rear end but mine was already pretty calloused by this point from my constant years of sitting.

Finally, we pulled up to one of the most serene places I've ever known. My outdoor experience had been pretty limited. It had been mostly camping in the back yard with my father and brothers around a campfire, roasting marshmallows. Real rugged stuff! The whole place smelled of pine and some sort of combination of animals. There were ducks and geese all over the place. Set back into this oasis of green rolling hills were eight log cabins, labeled from "A" to "H" that came into view as the buses rolled in and screeched to a halt.

As we got off the buses, it was utter chaos. Camp workers, all of whom were volunteers, were grabbing campers and wheelchairs left and right as if some mass kidnapping were taking place. Bags were flying overhead as each camper rushed to point out their wheelchairs among the zillions that came off the truck. I remember being lifted up from my bus seat and quickly shouting "That's my chair," so it would not get lost among the others.

My first thought when I arrived was that I looked nothing like these other campers. I was surprised to see all the people with different types of muscular dystrophy and how it had affected their lives. Now, I do not judge based on appearances, but what I saw was shocking. I saw physical differences that appeared worse than my own. I saw children wearing helmets and some with harnesses. I saw back braces, leg braces along with elaborate wheelchairs with modified backrests to accommodate their needs. It was almost strange to feel like the odd man out in a camp for children with disabilities, but I had never been aware of these levels of disability before. I did not know there were so many different levels. It took me two days before I could relax and be comfortable with my surroundings. I had never had another adult take care of me other than my parents or the occasional baby-sitter or family member. Not only did I feel shy, but it made other people uncomfortable or embarrassed to make mistakes. Sometimes people who don't know my limitations can hover and get scared and treat me like I'm more fragile than I really am. Each camper had an individual

Camp Counselors

counselor, and it took some time for mine to learn how able, as well as disabled, I really was.

Every day at meals, we would sing interactive and fun songs to music, like the Chicken Dance. You'd wiggle and clap and act out the song. Each cabin would have to come up with limericks depending on the day's theme. I was good at rhyming and loved coming up with limericks.

My favorite poem that I wrote was set to the music of I'm Proud to Be an American:

I'm proud to be at Camp MDA

Where at least I know I'm free.

I won't forget the volunteers

Who gave this right to me.

So, I gladly ride up next to you

To have fun here today.

There ain't no doubt I love this camp.

God bless the MDA.

Each cabin had a flag, and a camper would have to hold onto it throughout the day. If you lost it (that is, somebody stole it from you), you'd have to do whatever the other cabin requested to get it back. For example, dress up in dresses and make-up and put on a drag show; or shave the counselor's head; or clean somebody else's cabin. Sometimes we raided other cabins and left shaving cream, toilet paper and silly string everywhere. The usual consequence was revenge: The raided cabin would come back and raid you. After a raid, we'd spend hours cleaning up our cabins.

I especially loved fishing at camp, although going out on a dock with multiple wheelchairs flying about sometimes made me a bit nervous. Would I fall in? Would somebody hit me in? Would I fall backwards? It was a little scary. But all in all, it was wonderful to be out there on the lake on a beautiful sunny day, with all of the green and trees in the background. It was fun to compete against the other campers for the biggest fish, or the smallest fish, or the most fish! Over the years, I won several fishing awards.

On Thursday, we had Field Day. We had relay races, pie-eating contests, and tug-of-war. The police department brought K-9 dogs and showed us their skills. For the first time, it was a situation in which I could enjoy competition because we were at the same level.

The last day of camp, I became very sad. In fact, every year to come, I'd feel the same way. I felt very sad because now I knew I had to re-enter the "normal" world where people can be critical, judgmental and negative. MDA camp opened my eyes in a good way. Never before had I been so aware of what "disabled" meant. But if I finally understood what "disabled" actually meant, I also finally understood what it meant to be "normal." After all, "normal" is just being like everybody else, and at MDA camp, that's what we had.

I went back to MDA camp every year until I turned 18. From the moment I returned to my parents that first summer with a huge grin on my face and lots of stories to tell about my adventures, Mom and Dad were thrilled with MDA camp. They saw I was happy there and no longer feared for me. MDA was an oasis away from the cruel reality of the world and each year I looked forward to taking a break from the challenges of real life to find comfort with others who knew and shared my struggles.

My brother volunteers at camp

Chapter 8

MISS BETTY REMEMBERS

Betty S., a long-time Memphis resident, is a cheerful and energetic woman who works as a Family Care Specialist for the Mid-South Transplant Foundation. She started volunteering for the Muscular Dystrophy Association as a camp counselor when she was in high school. And then she just kept volunteering. Betty and I are still good friends.

Miss Betty always called the children "my babies." They were so little. At MDA camp, they would start out in her cabin

Miss Betty

and over the years work their way up to the big boys' cabins. It was amazing to watch them grow up; heartbreaking, too. Miss Betty had no kids of her own-they were her kids. She would volunteer for the Memphis Muscular Dystrophy Association and as an MDA camp counsel or/cabin director for the next 30 years.

For "her" babies, it was usually their first time away from home and the first few days were the hardest. Every year Miss Betty and the other volunteers would go up on Saturday before the kids arrived on Sunday morning. They'd get everything ready for them. We always had a theme with t-shirts and goody bags - this particular year it was cartoons. Out of the blue, my t-shirt turned out to be perfect! It had Speedy Gonzalez on it.

Miss Betty said I was just this itty bitty baby in this itty bitty wheelchair zooming around. They'd never seen a wheelchair that small. The other kids thought it was pretty cool. I'd invite them to stand on the back and ride around. Most of the other children with MD could walk at that age. My progression was different. I can remember Miss Betty saying, "There was not a shy bone in that boy's body." I was always very outgoing and very compassionate with the other kids. "And I always wanted to be the center of attention!" I wanted to do everything. I loved singing; I loved arts and crafts; I loved T-ball, fishing and singing karaoke and swimming! In the water, the other boys and I were free. Miss Betty said, "I would never allow his disability to stop him from doing anything. I credit Scott and Melisa for that" Miss Betty says, "he was amazing to watch; the wheelchair was really his legs."

Sometimes if I felt ornery, I'd just zoom off. My individual counselor would come to Miss Betty and say, "He's run off; he won't listen to me!" She would take my wheelchair out of gear by popping the clutch so I couldn't run off. That made me mad! If I got bored at meal time waiting for the older children to finish eating, I would just hit the door with my wheelchair,open it and run off. Ms. Betty would then make me sit with her. I hated that. I had a hard time with not being allowed to be alone.

Sometimes, if it even looked like I was getting bored, Miss Betty would pop my clutch. What I loved were the activities. If I wanted to do something, I would find a way to do it,no matter what. After dinner, when the boys would stand up on the tables to dance, I would go up to the front and do all of the Hokey Pokey moves with my wheelchair.

Miss Betty says she remembers once when she was on the floor, all the other little kids in the cabin started tickling her. I was in my wheelchair and couldn't reach her. So I said, "Miss Betty, let me sit on your stomach!" She thought I just wanted to be on the floor with the rest of the kids, but after she set me on her stomach, I made myself fall forward on her so I could tickle her, too. I could always find a way to be in the middle of things.

All the counselors were volunteers with other jobs and other lives. Miss Betty worked as an office manager for a doctor's office. Their volunteer nurse, Libby, worked for Dr. Berterini at the weekly muscular dystrophy clinic. So, Libby already knew a lot of the children. Only Norma, the director, was MDA staff. Norma was the heart and soul of MDA in Memphis. A lot of the individual counselors were high school students; in fact, Miss Betty started volunteering when she was a high school student. Some of the volunteers were Boy Scouts. A core group of them would come back to camp every year; it was incredibly special.

Miss Betty recalled, "The kids would arrive on these two big buses. All the equipment would be in a big moving van: wheelchairs, shower seats, hospital beds, everything. The kids would go crazy when they got off the bus. The counselors get everything sorted out, go to our cabins, and play get-to-know-you games. There were eight cabins, sorted according to age. Children could start MDA camp at six and keep coming till they were 21. Anywhere from 30 to 60 kids would come each summer. We had one girls' cabin and all the rest were for boys'. I always got along with the girls just as well as the boys. I was comfortable with everyone."

"We'd start out the day with breakfast, med check, first activity, then down time before lunch. There would be a different activity after lunch. Some of the older children, as the disease progressed, needed more breaks than the younger ones. Most of the older kids were in wheelchairs, and most of the younger children could walk. You might look at some of the little kids and never know anything was wrong; but maybe by the end of the night, they'd have a hard time walking. Some of the children weren't used to so much physical activity. They might be hurting and needing to get out of their wheelchairs, or they may be having trouble breathing from being in the wheelchair for so long."

"Not Evin, though. He never wanted to stop." For the little boys, there was no way they'd want to nap. They would always have goody bags: army men, parachutes and blow up balls. They'd play in our bunks or get on the floor. It wasn't uncommon for one of the boys to move stuff to where I couldn't reach it. "Evin and the other boys bonded; they were part of a core group that came back each year and moved up to the older boys' cabins together."

The kids lived for camp. It was Christmas, birthdays and holidays all rolled into one. Some of the kids were very poor. They didn't even have a suitcase, just a brown paper bag. They might only have one set of clean clothes and a change of underwear. The fundraising was important. MDA paid for the camp making it free for the campers. The counselors made sure every child went home with five sets of clothes, a toothbrush, a towel and a bathing suit! In my cabin, there was not one kid who didn't get what they needed.

"Everything at camp was adapted for the children. They got to feel normal; they got to do everything. They never wanted to leave. I remember how we were always looking for male counselors and Evin was maybe seven years old when he and I spoke at his dad's Marine Reserves unit …"

"Evin just sat there and talked about his disability and how important the camp was. These great big Marines were sitting there with tears in their eyes! He always had that ability to connect. There was never a question he couldn't ask you. He always gave 110 percent!"

"At camp, Norma was always looking for the next State Goodwill Ambassador. She thought that Evin was perfect. Evin was so cute and vocal, energetic and positive. And he had a supportive family. Melisa and I took him everywhere. Evin was the personal face of the MDA, first for the County and then for all of Tennessee. He'd go to police stations, military establishments, firehouses. "Fill the Boot" was a big campaign at firehouses. We did a lot of traveling. Evin was always getting his picture taken and he did the local telethon ever year. He was given the keys to the city, made an honorary deputy sheriff, and met with Penny Hardaway, the NBA basketball star, who helped us with fundraising. Evin says he was like the Miss USA of the Muscular Dystrophy Association. It wasn't all about fund raising, either. Evin would visit other disabled kids, comfort the parents, show them that disabled kids can still keep doing things and have a rich life."

Evin begins….

At the Jerry Lewis Labor Day telethon in Memphis, when we weren't on camera, I would go up to each operator on the break and introduce myself. I would ask their names and how they came to work the telethon. I'd tell them how important camp was and fund raising was and how the money actually helped. I'd say, "You see that boy over there? That's my friend Harry, and at camp, you can help him do arts and crafts. If we raise enough money, we might help Harry get a new chair or get a flu shot."

I made it my goal to meet every kid I didn't know and talk to them about coming to camp. I just wanted to give back. Several of the kids did come to camp, too. When I got a little older, I'd sit in my wheelchair in the middle of the risers and ask all the operators, "Do you have any questions?" and I'd tell them what an important job they were doing. When I met a firefighter, I'd say, "You need to come to camp. They need a man! You could lift that big boy over there. Next year, I'll come to your firehouse if you like." I liked to show people how much you could do as a disabled person. I never wanted anybody to feel sorry for me. Miss Betty credits my Mom and Dad. They never held me back; they always fought for me. They wanted me to do everything I could possibly do and more. I was always pushing the envelope.

My disease was different than some of the other children. Miss Betty says they didn't know the actual diagnosis then: Merosin's MD. It's rare. The most common kind is Duchene's. These kids seem perfectly fine at first; they can walk and run. But at around age five or six, they start falling down. I never walked, but my type of MD reaches a certain point and then stops progressing. Duchene's never stops. As they got a little older, when they'd go to stand up, they'd have to use their hands. They'd use a hand to pull a leg up. Then some who were not walking so much would have to throw a foot out to move forward. Then would come the braces. Then there'd be trouble holding heads up for periods of time or even at all. Then they would gradually have to graduate to a wheelchair. Maybe they can't lift their arms over their heads any more. At first, they could roll over in bed. Then they can't move their legs at all and then they can't roll over in bed any more. Maybe they'll have mobility in their arms only from the elbow down. Then they'll have trouble swallowing. It becomes hard to eat. Their arms don't work and they can't feed themselves. They can't even move in bed. They have to call someone if they need anything. They're in constant pain. They can't stay in a wheelchair for more than a couple of hours at a time; then they need to lie down. They develop problems breathing; can't get enough oxygen. And the heart starts to fail. By the time they're 15 or 16, they've lost everything.

My friend Lane is almost 21 and he has Duchene's. His heart and lungs are weak. He'd cheated death five times that I know of. Four years ago they said he had to get a ventilator. He said no. They changed his meds and breathing treatment, and he was able to get off his pain meds. He kept his oxygen levels up. But recently, they said he really had to get a vent. But he still said no. They told him he wasn't getting enough oxygen. He said, "I just don't want to live like that. If it's time for me to go, I'll go." His mother said it would kill her, but she'd do what he wanted her to do.

Sometimes with the vent, you can't talk. Lane told me his daddy and his uncle would take him hunting. He couldn't shoot but he could go along. For

Miss Hope's Chariot

graduation, he wanted a four-wheeling side-by-side "redneck-jeep" with big tire sandbars. He wasn't able to drive the four-wheeler but he could sit in it. Everybody had pitched in and gotten him one. Lane said, "If I get a vent, I can never ride in my side-by-side again. I'll never be able to go to the lake again. It's dusty, it's dirty and muddy." It would have taken away what little freedom he had.

I asked Miss Betty once if any of her "babies" had ever died. I was thinking about Liam. Liam, like Lane, didn't want to get a vent. His mom let him make the decision about it. She said, "OK, you realize if you don't have a vent, you will die?" He said, "That just means I'll meet Jesus sooner." He got worse. They still asked him about the vent and he still refused it. The last time, he was in severe respiratory distress. He wanted to die at home. His mom took him home. Miss Betty was there. She said, "OK, this is it. If you don't use a respirator, this is it." He just looked at her with a big smile and said, "It's time to see Jesus." He was dead within two hours.

My fight has been different. It's not about how I want to die, its about how I want to live. For me, it's all about fighting for independence; fighting for opportunity. It's about freedom.

Chapter 9

PLAYTIME

Goofing Off

In those early years, I did not feel isolated. My brothers were my playmates at home, and I loved to cuddle with my dog, Cinnamon. She was our dog after Beemer. I never related to Beemer much – he was too rough. Beemer was a 'Blue Heeler,' a kind of sheepdog that herds sheep into a pen. He was gray with some big black patches. When we first got him, he was a puppy; but by the time he was about a year old, his natural instincts kicked in and he would always try to herd me back toward the house. Normally, animals stay away from my chair. But if I got a certain distance from the house, Beemer would bite at my front tire and push his body on the side of my chair, trying to get me to go back. He was too rambunctious for me to play with him, though … he was more suited for Alex and Nathan.

But when Beemer was about 5 years old, we got Cinnamon from a good friend of my dad. Cinnamon was a very loving and truly gentle pit bull, all different shades of glossy brown, like a painting. She would come along side of me and put her head under my hand. She was very smart and could sense I needed gentleness. She was like a big lap dog.

My brothers and I spent most of our time playing in the backyard. Our backyard was your average Memphis backyard and we boys gave it an average beating. The grass was faded from a dark healthy green to a greenish gray because of how much we abused it. We had caramel-colored wooden fencing, with planks that alternated in such a way that if you were on the inside of it, it was possible climb and jump over. Cinnamon used to climb the fence, too. She climbed over it every time she got lonely in the backyard. Then she'd run around to the front door and sit there, waiting for somebody to come home.

My dad tried to do everything with me that he had done with Alex. He thought I should be able to have all the same experiences. Sometimes that was great; sometimes not so hot. One thing I loved to do was to be on the trampoline with my brothers. My dad would set me between his legs with his knees locked on either side of my body as we bounced up and down. I loved both the feeling of weightlessness, and playing and laughing so hard with my brothers. When it came to backyard camping. Dad said, "Hey, we're going camping, just you and me." I knew he went backyard camping with Alex, but I was skeptical. I said, "I don't know - sleeping on the ground …" It just sounded painful to me. But when the sun went down, Dad carried me out back. We had a campfire and made S'mores and Dad told me stories about the stars and the family and then spooky stories. Then he made me a "pallet" (I think that's a military term) with a blow up mattress, and we went to sleep. I think we made it until about midnight till he carried me back inside. It was fun, I have to admit.

Pool Time

But another time that was really awful was our camping trip when we went on in the mountains with my cousins. We went on this hike and they rigged up a kind of sling made out of a bed sheet hanging from two poles. That was used to carry me. It was terrifying. We went uphill and downhill and I was swinging back and forth, and forward and back. I felt like I was about to fall off the cliff any second. My foot kept getting banged backward because the sling wasn't really high enough and my feet stuck out. I screeched every time. Even though I can't move my feet very much, I can still feel them. I kept begging my dad to leave me by the side of the trail and come back for me. Of course, he wouldn't. Dad was happy he was including me on our family adventure but for me truthfully, it was pretty horrible.

My brothers and I spent a lot of time in our above ground pool. The summers in Tennessee were ridiculously hot. Almost every summer, the high would be from 100 to 110 degrees Fahrenheit, and sometimes it would go up even higher. It was a humid heat that would give you a sunburn before you started sweating. I was not actually able to swim in the pool, but with the help from my own natural buoyancy, the water was able to hold me up enough where I could hold on to the side and walk around on my toes. Despite the contractures that pulled tightly on my muscles, I had great balance. I could leave the edge of the pool, but at a cost. Because of my physical weakness, if I fell over, I couldn't pull myself back up. I got used to the waves my brothers made and I could lean into them, creating a counter-balance so they wouldn't knock me over. But I couldn't avoid every single wave. Because of this, I had to have somebody with me in the pool whenever I went in. It might be my older brother, or my mom or dad. However, whoever was in the pool with me didn't necessarily stand right next to me. If I were by the ladder or at the edge of the pool, I was secure. But when I fell over and went under, my heart would race. I knew someone was there, but I didn't know for sure if they were watching me. Eventually, somebody would come to my rescue, but in my mind, I was thinking: Hello, I'm drowning!! I was holding my breath, which was hard to do with my lungs, and I would think: Are you guys going to save me or what?

After they'd pull me up, I'd gasp for air and be placed over by the edge of the pool. Nobody would freak out … this is just what it's like to be disabled. This was my norm. I'd almost drown, get rescued, and then go on.

Because I was so young and dare devilish, I thought that I was invincible. But slowly, I began to understand what fear is … I began to understand that I could get

Camping

hurt; someone might not always be there to save me. And I began to get scared to be in or around around bodies of water. However, fear never stopped me, because regardless of how scared I was, I kept getting in the pool each summer. After almost drowning and being hauled up so many times, I did get a bit of PTSD. Whenever I was around any large body of water, even if I wasn't in it, I would become uncomfortable. It felt like I couldn't breathe - like I was already under water. My heart would start racing. I wanted to stay away, but I wouldn't let fear beat me.

One thing I loved about our circular above ground pool and miss to this day was when my dad and brother Alex would run around in circles. I would hold onto the ladder with my elbows and ankles around the ladder rungs. My dad and Alex, standing opposite to each other, would both run in the same direction at the outside edges of the pool. This would cause a whirlpool like effect, causing everything to spin faster and faster ... it reminded me of a toilet! When it got to a certain speed, they would stop and pick up their feet and let the water carry them around and around in circles. And I would let go of the ladder and the water would carry me as well. Because all the water was going in the same direction and at the same speed ... not sloshing from all directions ... I didn't have to worry about being knocked over. I would close my eyes and it felt as if I were gliding. When I started to slow down, I'd catch onto the ladder when it came around.

One day, when my cousin Lauren was visiting, she and Alex decided to create a whirlpool like we always did. I was holding onto the ladder and most likely I was saying, "Go faster." Instead of stopping at the usual speed, they just kept going faster and faster. This was when I learned about centrifugal force. Before I knew what was happening, the walls of the pool collapsed in every direction. It was too much pressure. The pool siding fell flat, and the water gushed everywhere, slinging Alex, Lauren and myself into the wooden fence. None of us was hurt and we all thought it was fun, and I wanted to do it again. I am pretty sure that we broke the pool and my Dad had to get another one.

ALEX HARTSELL

Alex, my older brother, goes by his middle name like my Dad does. He's a 31-year-old with a square chin and dark hair. Alex was also in the Marine Corps like my Dad. After the military he got a job working at an electrical contracting business as a Project Manager. Here's how he remembers growing up with me:

"Dad used to say that he had a new son issued with each new 3 year duty station. We were living in Tennessee, and that's where I live now with my wife Lindsey and my two boys, Logan and Titus."

"It's interesting, when you grow up in an environment like we did; it seems like the norm. It was the same thing day in and day out. Evin just had a chair. We communicated and played and fought like all other brothers. Evin would play; we'd integrate him into however we played. Evin would kick the ball with his chair. We'd just adapt to how it was. He was the same to us-not handicapped. It was just what we did. We'd have fights. He'd wham me with his wheelchair and I'd hit him back. Then he'd run figure-eights around me going "Ouch, ouch, ouch.""

"For me, nothing ever seemed out of place until about middle school and high school. That's when I started to feel more that there was something different."

"Evin would be taken to school by a special bus that was different from mine. I didn't want him to feel different or feel bad, and I'd ride with him. That was always my role. If Evin felt out of place, I would help and protect him. If Nathan and I saw anybody staring at Evin, would look at each other and just stare back."

"I remember, when I first noticed the way some other kids behaved. There was this one particular incident. There was a young boy down the street who was not all that friendly. His family seemed to have a lot of money. They had a pool and a trampoline. If Evin ever moved out of his wheelchair, this boy would take the wheelchair, just like it was a joke. He was going to just take it and drive off in it. It was supposed to be a joke,but it really bothered me."

"And one time, when Evin was about ten and I was about 13, Evin must have gotten out of the chair to play on the grass. So the boy wanted to take the wheelchair. Evin didn't feel so comfortable about it but he said yes. So the kid drove off like he was going to leave Evin sitting there. He went several houses down,and I had this epiphany,this moment of clarity. It dawned on me that Evin couldn't defend himself. Hey, Evin can't chase that kid down! He really is different. That kid was using his strength to take advantage of Evin. I stopped the boy and made him get out of the chair. No one messes with my brother! It was a defining moment for me. When I see people taking advantage of others, I get very angry. It's a big part of why I joined the Marines. I don't like bullies - people who take advantage. You have to stand up for people who can't stand up for themselves. You have to make sure others don't feel excluded."

Evin offers...

I was five when I met my best childhood friend, Patrick Brooks. He lived three houses down, on the same street to the left. Except for the kids at camp, my friends were more like acquaintances – there were none who immediately looked past my disability. But Patrick did. Patrick was small enough that he could ride on the back of my chair. He would stand on the battery that stuck out behind as we zoomed from house to house. Or he would put on his skates and I would fling him around as we zipped all over the neighborhood. That was another fun thing: other children, whether we knew them or not, would line up or just create a link-like chain behind my chair as we sped along.

There was a different atmosphere in the Brooks' home. It wasn't a military-religious home like ours. Not to say it wasn't disciplined or unloving. Just more freedom than what I was used to. Because of the date of Patrick's birthday, he was a year behind me in school. But this didn't hold us back from hanging out and discussing school-related events. Patrick and I would hang out about three or four times a week. We would play outdoors or play video games.

Over the years, we became so close that when he was 16, he volunteered to be my personal counselor at MDA camp. The person who was supposed to do it couldn't go at the last minute. I wouldn't have been able to go to camp otherwise. Patrick did everything for me: helped me get dressed, eat, go to the bathroom, and get into my wheelchair. He says he never understood or appreciated how much my parents had to do for me until then. For Patrick, the only difference between us was that I had a wheelchair. When we were young, the wheelchair was just like an additional toy.

I like to joke and rib him about something that happened when we were nine. It was a hot day outside and to avoid the heat,we decided to play in the empty garage. My motorized wheelchair had run out of power, and while it was charging, Patrick started pushing me around in a manual wheelchair, which wasn't as sturdy. Patrick was excited and he started running around in circles,pushing me faster and faster. Suddenly, Patrick, in all his excitement, turned too quickly. The chair tipped to one side and toppled over and the front right side of my head hit the concrete. I was out before I knew what had happened! Patrick said,"Evin are you okay?" With no response coming from me, he became very nervous and panicked. He ran home and left me there unconscious without calling for any help. Luckily, Patrick's six-year-old brother Hunter was there when it happened. After Patrick ran away, Hunter opened the garage door to the house and yelled, "MRS. HARTSELL, EVIN'S DEAD!" Then he ran home, too. My mother came out to the garage and found me lying on the floor. She was scared; she didn't know what had happened. But, as Mom says, "Evin fell over all the time … so it wasn't something new." I woke quickly. She carried me into the living room and watched me to make sure I didn't have a concussion. I remember lying in the living room with a big lump on my forehead. My mom called Patrick's mom to let him know I was all right. I could hear Patrick crying in the background over the phone. He was saying, "I killed my best friend! I killed my best friend!" He says he was traumatized for days afterward.

I think that was the first time I noticed how much he cared about me. I love this story because every time I tell it, even today, Patrick blushes and gets an embarrassed look on his face. It reminds both of us how close we actually are. I know today I wouldn't be where I am without a best friend like Patrick -- he kept me sane for many years! These days, according to Patrick, I don't talk about death as much as I used to. He says I talked about dying the whole time I was growing up. He thought I was worried about it, but actually, I wasn't. For the longest time, the doctors would say: You weren't supposed to live this long! When I passed the age the doctors said I'd die, I said: They don't know how long I'm going to live. There's no precedent. Finally I just said: Hey, I'm still alive. The heck with it. I wasn't worried about death. I just wanted to remind people so they wouldn't be freaked-out if I died suddenly. Little kids are traumatized so easily. And I wanted to make every second count. Let's live! I had friends dying all around me. Let's enjoy what we have while we have it!

My other "best friend" wasn't a real person: It was video games. I remember the first time I saw a video game. I must have been six years old. My brother Alex was playing "Sonic the Hedgehog" and "Zelda, Ocarina of Time." It was amazing to me. I loved how fast Sonic could go … because without my chair I was so slow. I loved the sounds and the special effects. It was fun to be able to speed around in a game and not have to worry about falling over. It was unlike speeding around in a chair, falling over and bruising everything – which seemed to happen more and more often. Zelda, Ocarina of Time,was the first fictional world I remember experiencing but due to my age it was way over my head. It was a whole world full of whimsical characters and interesting bad guys.

At first, the thrill of games was incredibly overwhelming. Once I got more used to them, video games gave me a way to compete, something to strive to beat. They were a big help, although maybe they held me back, too. I could always escape my problems into video games. As I grew older, they became a much-needed source of comfort. Video games were the one thing that could distract me from my ever-growing depression.

When I went to school, I didn't make a lot of new friends who would come over to the house. But I made one special friend who is still my friend to this day. Her name was Katricia, and she was my assistant in school.

Neighbor Friends Patrick and Hunter

Chapter 10

ONE-ON-ONE

Katricia T. shares her memory and her thoughts on her 11 years of working with me as my personal school assistant, my mentor and my friend:

"I was hired by the school district when I was 26 years old and Evin was my very first assignment. He was in second grade. I was hired to be his one-on-one assistant and I was him continuously each day at school. Sometimes in the summer, I'd also babysit for Evin at his home. He was like my own boy. I'd call him my son. When I first met him, I thought oh my goodness, I don't know how to work with him. I thought he was super-fragile. I later found out he was a tough kid."

Personal School Assistant

"Evin was very manipulative. To get out of work, he'd push his pencil off the desk and then he'd say he couldn't get his work done. I was constantly sharpening pencils. I didn't realize that he was manipulating me. It took a while. Finally, I caught him pushing a pencil off the table. Oh no, I thought, not this little sweet innocent child with a disability! I couldn't believe it. He had to learn to be like every body else. His teacher, Miss C., would take a rest room break but Evin would say no, he didn't have to go. Then in the middle of the lesson, Evin would have to go. Miss C. started noticing it. Finally, we said, 'No, you have to go when everybody else goes.' Evin didn't like it. But he got used to it."

"We found a mutual ground in singing. We were outside one time at recess. Evin always stuck by me at first. I started singing, 'Jesus loves me, this I know.' Evin sang too. He loved to sing. That's when he knew I went to church, and we had that in common. I told him my dad was a pastor. He taught me a little song that he knew which helped him to remember the books of the Bible. "Was

Elementary School

he polite in second grade? Not always. But he was afraid what people would say or think about him. I think Evin's a genius. He is very smart. His body doesn't work with his brain. He had a slick tongue! He would get you, and you'd say, Wow, really? He could be disrespectful sometimes, but I'd just walk away because he hated to be ignored."

"The administration tried to put Evin into special education as soon as he entered elementary school. I was not invited to the meetings, but Evin's parents fought it. They fought it, tooth and nail. His disability was physical, not mental. He still had an IEP, (Independent Educational Program), but he was in the regular classroom."

"After Evin went on to middle school, his parent again had a big fight on their hands to keep him out of the"Resource Room" and in the mainstream classroom."

"Sometimes he'd just shut down. I'd say, 'What's wrong?' He wouldn't say. Finally, he'd tell me: These kids said this or that; they were looking at me! I'd say: 'That's cause you're so handsome!' Mostly this happened in elementary school; he was the only kid in school with a wheelchair. But once the kids got to know him, they realized he wasn't fragile. I'd encourage Evin to get into different groups. He'd participate. He started talking more and joking around and then they'd talk and joke around with him."

"I gave him the nickname that stuck with him all his life - Speedy. He liked to go fast on that electric wheelchair. Once, I had to do a project in college that involved going into a store in a wheelchair to see how people with a disability were treated. I realized then that people weren't so helpful. The kids at school were the same way. Evin would be in the hallway and he'd say: 'Excuse me.' They'd be standing around, but they wouldn't move. I'd be thinking: Why don't these kids see that he's in a wheelchair and could just run them over? I told Evin: 'Here's what you do. Say excuse me three times and if they don't move, go for the gusto. I'd go behind him and I'd call out, 'Here comes Speedy! That's right, get out of his way."

"Later on, when he was in middle school, fifth grade I think, the principal and I were talking about the National Anthem PA system. And I said, "Hey, can we sing it?" I was just kidding around; I didn't even know if Evin knew the national anthem. But the principal said yes. So, I asked Evin if he could sing it and he said he could. We practiced first and then we started singing it together, over the loudspeaker. Halfway through, I stopped singing so Evin had to keep going by himself. That's when I found out he has a really beautiful voice. After that, he joined the chorus. I'd go to see him whenever there was a performance."

"Evin had a beautiful voice that developed into a rich tenor as he got older. He participated in chorus for many years. His dad was so proud of him. We'd go to his performances and you could hear that sweet voice. His dad would say, 'Oh my goodness!' His parents were so happy that he found something that he could do with the other kids, something that he excelled at. "The other chorus members and the school, they all helped Evin, getting into his uniform, holding the music." They modified the back stage to be able to get the wheelchair up on it. "He was just one of the gang; it was good for him,".

"I helped Evin push past what he thought was his limit. I wouldn't let him quit. He'd get frustrated with something, maybe his work, and say, 'I can't, I can't.' And I'd say, 'It's your body that's not working, not your brain. I have a very strong spiritual background and I knew Evin did too, so when he said 'I can't,' I'd ask, 'What does the Bible say? I can do all things through Christ who strengthens me. Now do you want to be a winner or a quitter? Or sometimes I'd say, 'Oh you can't?' And I'd walk over to another student and I'd ask, 'Can you do this?' And the other student would say yes. So Evin would say: 'If he can do it, I can do it.' Sometimes I'd just bribe him with candy. Skittles. We really did eat too much candy, I have to say that."

"He was so good at math, that they started refusing to allow me to test him. They wouldn't let me test him – for anything. They thought I was giving him answers! I said that was pretty funny because if I were giving him the answers, he would not be getting the answers right. They would remove me whenever he had to take tests and place him with someone else. I wasn't the kind of person who would cheat. Ever!" "Evin had to take a Tennessee CAP test, which is a standardized test. They didn't trust me to administer it to him, so they put us in a room with a proctor. I sat at one desk with the answer sheet and Evin sat at another desk with the test. The proctor leaned over Evin's shoulder while he was reading. He didn't need any help reading. Then Evin would just call out the answer to me: A, or B, or C. "After a while, the proctor started walking around the room. 'So why am I here?' he asked. " 'I don't know," I said. 'All he's doing is telling you A, B, C or D. 'I know,'I say. We had to do that an hour a day for four days because they had a hard time believing Evin was really so good at math."

"Evin was like one of my own children. I babysat for him in the summer time, especially when he was in middle school. Evin got close to my kids when I would bring them along whenever I would go to his house to baby sit."

"When Evin graduated to middle school, the district told us that he was going to be reassigned. Evin would no longer have one-on-one school help. The district wanted to put him into special education. I always wondered if there was something about her that made the school want to separate. I fought it tooth and nail. I was very outspoken on his behalf," I made sure Evin got what he needed. It wasn't an issue for the principal but maybe it was for some of the teachers. I wondered if I was too pushy. They thought I was doing his work! As an explanation, the district told me that females could not work with male students. "But that was a lie, because they put me with another male student in another school.

"We fought it," but we didn't win. "The Hartsells felt the change was just due to financial concerns that the school had about having to pay for Evin separately from the other students. And the school didn't really understand Evin. According to the Hartsells, the district had never dealt with a physically disabled person like Evin before, and they didn't know how to handle it."

"The only handicapped bathroom was in the "resource room,"which was the room for all of the Special Education kids, and the Resource Room was on the other side of the school from the regular classrooms. In other words, the only handicapped bathroom in the school was on the other side of the school from all of the regular classrooms. So that made it difficult for Evin to be in mainstream classes without a one-on-one helper. Who would take him to the bathroom?

And where would he have lunch? Somebody had to feed him. Where would he go for recreation?"

"Melisa thought the school just didn't understand Evin's intellect' but Scott thought it was all about money. The school's budget was set up to have a certain number of aides in the resource room. And if they took one of them out to stay with Evin, it would cost more money. Scott believed that the school was trying to keep Evin in a certain physical location because of his physical needs. But most of the kids in there source room had some kind of mental or emotional issues, like ADHD or autism. Mentally, they were having a hard time. That wasn't Evin. He didn't fit in, and his lessons were not up to the level of his ability. Melisa felt the school had to be educated and enlightened about Evin even in elementary school. It was as if the school saw a seriously disabled body and believed Evin's mind must be disabled, too. The struggle continued for several years before Evin was successfully mainstreamed. The Hartsells would get him out of the resource room, and after a while, he'd end up there again. Then the fight would start all over again."

"Evin joined choir, chess and scouts - as many activities as the Hartsells could find to enrich his life and show the school how capable he really was. I continued to help Evin at home throughout middle and high school. Later, when the Hartsells moved away, I lost touch for years. I was afraid. I wanted see how Evin was doing, but I was afraid I would hear the bad news. My daughter encouraged me to try. Finally through a friend of Evin's, I found his mother. Since then, Evin and I keep in contact."

"I just think he's a very great inspiration to everyone, disability or not. I'm really clueless as to why some people fail to connect with Evin. He doesn't allow his limitations to limit him. He works with what he has. I'll still say he's my son. That's my child! I didn't give birth to him, but that's my child."

Chapter 11

SOMEDAY I WILL BE A NORMAL BOY

Mom and Dad supporting Me

I believed there would be a cure. I believed that someday, I would walk around like a normal person. Even after I had a full spinal fusion at age 12.

Like most kids with MD, I had severe scoliosis. Scoliosis is the curving and twisting of the spine. The spine actually curves around in your back like a snake, and it twists your ribs and pelvis and compresses your chest around your lungs and heart. It can even cause your ribs to rub internally on other parts of your body, which can cause all sorts of problems. The doctors had been talking to my parents about a full spinal fusion since I was nine, but once I had the surgery, I would not grow any taller. My friend Gavin (the one who also has Merosin's MD) didn't get his spinal fusion until recently, when he was 16.

But by the time I was 11, the scoliosis was making it hard for me to breath. One lung was being crushed and other organs were being pushed and pulled. That's when we realized it was time. I don't remember if I was nervous. I do remember being wheeled into the surgery room and having a mask put over my face and drifting off to sleep. They sliced me open like a piece of sushi from neck to butt and placed two rods in my back. Then they attached the rods to my vertebrae with screws. It not only straightened my spine, but also kept it from twisting and rotating any more than it already had. As I healed, the bones of my own vertebrae would grow together, or "fuse."

When I woke up, the doctors said the operation was a complete success. The wound hurt but for the most part, I was more comfortable than I'd ever been. I felt relief from my rib cage. I no longer felt like I was being crushed by my own bones.

I was never a fan of hospitals. The air is too cold, which makes my muscles hurt, and the food is terrible. And I couldn't wait to get back to school. I asked the doctor how long it would take for me to heal up. He said, "It'll be about six weeks." I laughed and said, "I'll be out of here in a week." I was used to people thinking they knew me and what I was capable of. The doctor smiled and said, "That's not going to happen." I smiled and said, "Watch me!" It was great to prove the doctor wrong. In one week, I was out of the hospital. I was home for one more week, and then I was back in school. The doctors said they had never seen a full spinal fusion patient recover as fast as I had. I had never felt straighter and more comfortable physically thus far in my lifetime. But mentally, things were changing.

I began to notice and care about the subtle and not so subtle differences. Other kids were doing things that I realized I couldn't do. Something as simple as climbing a tree or riding a bike was beyond me. While my brothers would help dad change the oil in the car, I sat watching on the side. That is how I felt my life was going. I was just a bystander watching from the side lines as everyone else lived their lives.

At 12 years old, thinking about living a life with a disability was overwhelming. I just couldn't do it. I believed that a cure would come along. So I thought I didn't have to learn how to live a life with a disability because I was going to be cured! Out of kindness, people would down play how hard my life was going to be. Some people would say, "If you try really hard you can accomplish anything." When people told me I could achieve anything, I didn't think: Evin, you're going to have to do it differently. I thought I could. I would ride a bike. I would climb a mountain … using my arms and legs!

Looking back, I really wish someone had prepared me by saying that my life was going to be hard and painful. And that I could do things that everyone else did, but not in the same way. They should have said: "Don't stop fighting.

That's no reason to quit. You can do it, but you've got to find your own way!" That might have given me realistic expectations and goals. Instead, I put a lot of energy towards the impossible. Still until this day, I hate the word 'hope.' Hope was crippling me. That was my hope - a cure. Everybody has a fantasy when they're younger: maybe to be rich, to be an athlete, or to have a smoking-hot girlfriend. I wanted all that too, but a cure for my disability underlay it all. That was the primary plan - to wait for the cure.

Back then, my parents believed there would be a cure, too. There was so much great research going on, especially at the MDA: stem cell research, genetic research, and blood work. We all thought there would be something. My mom says, "Well, you have to have hope. When you live without hope, what do you have?" She didn't know what the future held. Before we connected with the MDA and other families with MD, she says she didn't really believe that I would die young. It wasn't until she saw other children dying that reality began to sink in. She says, "Your dad and I were both guilty of hoping for something that would possibly never come."

My parents were always trying to show me how much was available to me, even as a disabled person. They took me everywhere. There was talk about college. They were always pushing me to do things that other kids my age were doing.

But by the time I was 12, my life was going down hill. When we would sit together to eat dinner, Dad used to make everybody share something good that happened to you that day with the rest of the family. By the time I was 12, I was working really hard to be contrary. I'd think of something bad that happened and say it was something good, just to push back. I was turning into one of those obnoxious teenagers.

Other than Patrick and my brothers, I didn't have much social interaction with peers to help me grow socially. Most of my interactions were with adults or children way younger than me. I began being unable to discern what was appropriate to say to other kids my age.

When you start puberty, never being able to be alone is hard. It's not like I could just go off and explore my neighborhood. I couldn't close my door and just have "private time." I couldn't get away with anything. I couldn't sneak sweets from the fridge, stay up late at night, or even just go off alone.

Gaming in the hospital

When my parents said it was time to eat, I ate. When my parents said it was time to sleep, I went to bed. Eyes were constantly on me. There was nothing I could do independently, just like when I was two years old. Because I couldn't rebel, I didn't think independently. Because I felt I had no control, I began to misbehave. I began to lie. Like most young people, I might lie or manipulate to get a piece of chocolate or not eat string beans. But I began to lie in places I didn't need to lie. It was my way of asserting some control. Metaphorically, it was a way I could give people the finger.

I'd say, "Nate said a curse word!"when he hadn't. I'd make up stuff. For example in school, somebody would ask if I'd seen something, and I'd say yes and then describe a made-up scenario without knowing what I was talking about at all. If I said, "Two oranges plus two oranges equals 16 oranges," and somebody said, "What? That equals four oranges," I'd say "Yeah, well I meant if you cut up each orange into four parts, you end up with 16." I would tweak everything I said so I could always be right.

Aside from my parents, no one would call me on my bad or immature behavior. So while other kids my age were being reprimanded for their actions by teachers, neighbors and friends, or suffering the natural consequences of their own behavior, I was able to cry and pretend like life was too hard. And I started to believe that how I acted was socially acceptable. It got so bad, I started lying about my own lies. I'd actually forget I lied five minutes ago and believe in my own lies! Lying became second nature and it caused a rift between me and the few people who really cared about me. No one at home and at school would believe anything that I said, even if it was honest and true.

At 12, I wasn't at the point yet where I was pissed off or depressed all the time but I seemed to have no choices. I could see no path to achieve my dreams. I was still dreaming of a life without a disability. My friends were becoming more active. I found that fewer and fewer of them would stop and wait up for me. It hurt my feelings every time they did this. My wheelchair is fast but I still had limitations that simply slowed me down.

At that age, it's hard to put your self in someone else's shoes; I couldn't understand why they were leaving me behind. Was it because they didn't like me anymore, or they felt like I was a burden, or was it simply they didn't want to accommodate for me because it was too much trouble? I just wanted to know why. When the other kids started to avoid me socially, I began to feel like an outcast. Mom remembers the first time, when I was 13, I refused to go to a school dance. I felt I didn't have anything in common with anybody. I believe that the idea that (out of respect!), you couldn't talk about, or ask questions about my disability or that you should ignore it, or treat me like I am "normal" was creating a wall. In fact, I couldn't deal with all of the same things in the same way. I really am different.

Most of my peers, especially teenagers, never learned to ask about my disability. They were taught to ignore it. (Today, when I hear, "Don't stare! Don't ask rude questions!" I roll my eyes.) Unlike young children, who ask out of harmless curiosity, teens and adults are afraid. The other teens saw my wheelchair, but they didn't really understand what my true limitations were. Who is actually taught how to interact with a disabled person? I was even taught not to stare or ask questions out of respect. But how can you learn if you don't ask questions? The lesson "don't ask questions" is not a great one. I would prefer people of all ages ask me as many questions as they want. The more they ask, the more comfortable we get.

My disability can't be ignored. My disability is part of who I am. Without it, I am not Evin. If people saw my disability was a part of me, instead of a curse or weakness, maybe they would ask questions: Can you keep up? What is it you can and cannot do? What makes it hard for you? How can I change what I'm doing to make it easier for you?

Sometimes being treated as "normal" can be helpful... especially for someone who does not want help. For example, I notice people who become disabled later in life will go through hell to keep what little bit of "normal" they still have. Those are the people who might yell and say I don't need your help. It may be they're having a hard time coping with the loss. By treating them as "normal," it may help them to cope and give them more of a feeling of dignity. But for people who have been disabled from birth, who seem more comfortable with disability, treating them as "normal" can be harmful. "Normal" means conforming to whatever the standard is as measured by your peers. Normal is established by society. Normal means being pretty much like the majority.

"Equal" means the same opportunity-no bias, respect of the same value and merit. It has nothing to do with "normal." But at that time, I didn't know how to say any of this. I just started to withdraw. I began to give up on myself and on life.

Chapter 12

PUBERTY

When most people look at a disabled person in a wheelchair, the last thing they probably think about is sex. But disabled people have as much sexuality as anybody else. As an adolescent, I had powerful sexual feelings just like every other adolescent. Being disabled and going through puberty was overwhelming. I wanted a girlfriend, to eventually get married and have a family like everybody else. But how could that ever happen for me?

My parents never gave me the sex talk. I guess they figured I'd never have sex so why go through all that uncomfortable stuff? But for me, it was really tough. There was no book called Puberty for the Handicapped. Growing up in a religious home, we never openly talked about sex. Anytime this topic was brought up, all I would hear is, "You're supposed to wait until you are married." There was tons out there for me to learn, but I was cut off from the rest of the world.

Then something really awkward started to happen ... or at least, I thought it was awkward at the time. I don't any more. I began to realize I was not sexually attracted to girls. I was becoming attracted to males. The awareness started at the onset of puberty, and I struggled with it. Could I possibly be gay? How could I be gay as well as disabled? It seemed like it was too much for one person to shoulder and it made me feel bitter toward God.

Due to my Christian up bringing, I struggled with the idea that being gay meant I was diseased or cursed. I could not understand why I was attracted to men, even though I did not want to be. I thought: How could God do this to me? It added an extra layer to my growing depression. I was now not only depressed by my physical condition, but I was also depressed by these thoughts.

I had been taught that being gay was a choice. At this time in my life, I did not know that part of being gay is not a choice. I wanted to go to my church and ask for help but I had seen what happens when someone comes out with a secret like this. It wasn't good.

I tried to work on it myself. I thought it was my fault that my hormones were causing me to be attracted to males. I started resenting and hating God because I had been told that He won't give us more than we can handle. I began to withdraw from the church. I had witnessed how judgmental and disappointed fellow Christians could be when someone acknowledged a situation like mine and asked for help. In fact, it wasn't until I was about 19 years old that I finally told anybody. The very first person I told about my fears and thoughts about my sexuality was my father's sister, Aunt Karen. Aunt Karen is gay and a Christian. She does not believe that there's anything incompatible about being gay and being a good Christian. I was visiting her and decided to open up.

Aunt Karen is a very cool person who has been gay since she was a young woman. She was very supportive. I told her I thought I might be gay but I hadn't acted on it or anything. She said being gay was something you were born with, not something you chose. She'd been attracted to other females since she was very young. "I'm not going to live somebody else's life," she said. "It's my life." She didn't try to conform. Other people in our family, they tried to conform and be straight– unsuccessfully. But she didn't believe it was wrong to be gay. Recently, we were talking about being Christian and being gay and she said, "I don't have a problem with it at all. I don't think the Bible says it's a sin to be homosexual. That's other people's interpretation." I told my mother next. She was skeptical. She thought since I didn't have any experience with sex, how could I know? But when I told her I liked looking at gay porn on line, she sort of decided maybe I knew what I was talking about.

At the time, there was no way I could talk to my father about all of this. For a long time, even into my early 20s, I was afraid of my father, and at times I was intimidated by him. He was never actually violent, but he could get angry and get loud. When I was little, I actually feared he might hurt one of us and it gave me nightmares. So there was no way I was talking to Dad about it. Mom told Dad about my sexuality, but I'm not sure it sank in.

Over the years, I got more comfortable with who I actually was and how I felt. And I stopped being afraid of my father. Today, Dad and I have a much closer and more open relationship.

Even so, I only recently openly discussed my sexuality with both of my parents together. It was kind of funny. Even though Mom doesn't have a problem with it, I could see she was trying to 'protect' Dad.

Me: *When I was 13, did you notice at all the sexual struggles I was going through?*

Mom: *Well I remember, who was that little girl you had a crush on?*

Me: *That was like Kindergarten. I was six!*

Dad: *No. I never noticed that you ... your expression of sexual interest one way or the other. At all. I never saw it.*

Mom: *Well, little girls. He was interested in little girls.*

Dad *Yeah.*

Mom: *Yeah.*

"Silence"

Me: *Then I hid it well, huh? Okay.*

Mom: *Yeah, you did hide it cause I didn't know.*

After mentioning how, as an adolescent, I'd get aroused seeing men, I started to feel sorry for Dad, and I finally changed the subject.

But back when I was 13, all I really wanted was Dad's approval. For example, when I was little, I liked to play with Barbie dolls. My mother thought it was no big deal, but my dad did not approve. When I was 13 years old, my dad made it known that it was time for me to get rid of my dolls. By then I was much more into video games than dolls, anyway. So I didn't care. But instead of just throwing Barbie away, I wanted to make a statement of how over Barbie I was.

That's when Wedding Barbie happened – the start of a great family tradition that came out of my father's more "judgmental" attitudes. The Fourth of July was around the corner what better way to signify I'm over Barbie than to blow up my doll? It may be that I'm a bit of pyromaniac, because I was pretty excited about choosing a Barbie dress that would burn the best. I chose my favorite - the wedding dress!

Dad often had to miss holidays because of his military career and traveling with his civilian job. Even though he was in the Reserves, it was after 9/11 and he had to go away often. But the year I was thirteen, my Dad was home for the 4th of July and it was exciting. Dad, my brothers and I went out back. We tied Wedding Barbie to a Fourth of July rocket. Then we shot her off into the night sky. It was a great success. The next year, I made a Handicapped Barbie, with a mini-wheelchair, and shot her off into oblivion. We created a few more. Trailer-Park Barbie. When my brother's wife got pregnant, she suggested creating Pregnant Barbie for that year's Fourth.

It didn't change my sexuality, but it was kind of funny. The best of these celebrations was several years later when I was 18. Dad was called back on Active Duty again for a year to go to Afghanistan. My Aunt Karen and my Dad's brother, Uncle Mark, were visiting. We all went out to shoot off Taliban Barbies. By then, we were shooting off a number of Barbies in a themed production. That year, we dressed the Barbies with scraps of cloth to look like Taliban in honor of Dad's service, and we took them out to a nearby field to shoot them off on rockets. Then the whole field caught on fire. "Oh, crap, where's the fire extinguisher?" shouted Aunt Karen. "Evin, get in the van," everybody shouted. Of course I couldn't get in the van by myself; I couldn't move. But I was laughing. One of my nurses, Jennifer, was there and she got me into the van. Somebody shouted to my Uncle Mark to pee on the fire. He started stamping on it, and his pants caught on fire. My mom tackled him to make him roll so the fire would go out.

We all got into the car and quickly drove away - all except for Aunt Karen who stayed to greet the fire department. She said, "I don't know what happened, Officer." She had soot all over her face. I'm not sure exactly what happened next; and to this day, I still don't know why she wasn't arrested. We made a second Taliban Barbie with a full beard and mailed it to my dad in Afghanistan. We told him the story of what had happened to the first one. He loved it and said everyone he showed it to got such a good laugh. That helped relieve some of the stress that he and his fellow soldiers were going through as a result of being in a war and being separated from their families.

Taliban Barbie

Chapter 13

I MIGHT AS WELL BE DEAD

High School Chamber Choir

I vividly remember sitting in eighth grade English class, staring at the blackboard and thinking: Why am I even listening to the teacher? Why am I putting forth so much effort to achieve something that I will never achieve, since I'll never live a normal life? I didn't know any disabled adults who could advise me. I just sat there thinking: If I'm just going to be stuck at home after 12th grade, and if my life is over at18, why am I trying so hard? I couldn't picture being my own person. Most of my decisions were not my own. I was coddled and taken care of by people who only wanted to help. I felt I was good for nothing. Every time I'd struggle, someone would either help or actually complete my task. People seemed to think I couldn't do anything for myself.

To be honest, looking back, if the positions were reversed I would have behaved the same as the other kids did. I wanted to stare at people, to ask questions, and be in everyone else's business. Just because I'm disabled doesn't mean I'm not curious. I don't blame anybody for staring or for ignoring me. Because others were so darn helpful, I wasn't learning. It started to dawn on me: Holy crap, I can't do anything!

When my depression started, about age 12, I simply felt sad, or blah, like when it's raining outside. It was a feeling of boredom that would come and go throughout the week though I was still excited about things and loved my life. This phase lasted for about six to eight months. In the next phase, which lasted for about four months, I was sad every day. I woke up sad; I went to bed sad. It wasn't just a couple of times a week; it was a constant struggle. I would do activities that brought me joy during part of my day, but despair in the end would always be there to swallow me again.

Being left behind by my peers, and having nothing to talk about or share, created more and more distance. Sharing experiences is what brings people closer together and the fewer experiences I could share, the more distanced I felt. I found fewer and fewer opportunities to start up a conversation because I had no relevant experiences or topics. As I got older, I figured out that there were hobbies and activities for me. But at this age I couldn't see them because I kept looking at things from a non-disabled' point of view. I still hadn't accepted the possibility that I would be disabled for the rest of my life.

When I was younger, video games were just for fun and entertainment. Now, games were a necessary distraction, an outlet. Without them, I don't know if I'd be here today. I began to doubt everything I'd ever heard, that I could do certain things, that I could do anything. I felt like a victim of disability. I didn't know what was really holding me back.

I started becoming sarcastically morbid, trying to trick myself into not caring about my disability. My sarcasm seemed to make people laugh and feel more comfortable around me. What they didn't know was that many times I wasn't joking. When I said "Don't worry, it's not like I'll die in a couple of days," not many knew that, in fact, I had friends all around me dying of muscular dystrophy and nobody knew how long I'd live.

By the time I was about 14, I came to expect others to avoid me. Avoidance became the norm because I could no longer converse with others; we could no longer relate. It was around this time depression began to seriously affect my life, and it went on for years. As my depression progressed, so did my sarcastic and disrespectful behavior. My experience was constantly out of touch with reality. People tiptoed around me.

According to my parents, up until the age of 11 or 12, I'd been a fairly loving and obedient child. But my behavior progressed from small misdeeds to disrespect and insults. We've all met someone disabled with terrible manners, and we just assume they are in a bad mood because of their disability. I've come to realize that their rudeness possibly originates from the way they were raised. Not how we are raised by parents but how we are raised by society.

My dad has a funny story (funny ironic, not funny ha ha) about how we would all be at a MDA event with other families, like a picnic or a Christmas party and (according to Dad) some of the teenagers were pretty awful. They were angry and sarcastic or sometimes disengaged and quiet. They would sometimes lash out verbally to get attention. He thought there was something wrong at home with these kids. Maybe they didn't have a good home life or their parents were struggling. He thought probably their parents weren't doing enough with their kids. Dad was so glad that I wasn't like that and I guess he thought I never would be either. Little did he know!

My negative way of thinking carried over into other aspects of my life such as school. Instead of trying to do my own work, I began to expect other people to do my work for me. Whenever I was tired or showed that I was having a hard time, people would just start helping me, as if they were obligated. This caused me to believe that when you are disabled, you truly don't have to do as much. I became complacent and lazy. I began manipulating my assistants to feel sorry for me, which lead them to do my work for me.

Sometimes people say, "I wish I could get someone to do my work for me," but for me all this really led to was my feeling stupid and left behind. I would be doomed to struggle with simple school work such as spelling or history. Even though most people seemed to like me, I could not relate to any group. I was an outsider. Now my friends stopped hanging out with me not only because of my physical limitations, but also because of my mental and emotional limitations. I felt useless. I was so bored that I actually wanted to do chores. Really, I just wanted to be useful and needed. I wanted responsibility. But I wasn't able to understand or verbalize that.

Having been raised in a Christian, military family, I was taught by my parents not to give up or quit. But high school was one of the roughest parts of my life. I was very depressed and bitter. It was when I felt the most separated from the world. People started dating, driving cars for the first time, preparing for their future jobs ... but not me. I felt like I wasn't accomplishing anything or progressing in life. Every morning, I woke up expecting that this day would be my last. Every night, I cried myself to sleep. I would wake up each morning wondering: Why bother?

Many people saw that I was smiling and looked happy. But deep down, I wanted it all to end. I was tired of the same old routine. I tried distracting myself with extracurricular activities, mainly choir. I also spent much of my time playing video games. Not because I loved playing the games anymore; not even because they helped me escape reality; they just helped me to waste time until the end.

My depression was progressing like a virus. I had no choice but to keep these dark feelings to myself. I knew there wasn't anyone on earth who could fix me the way I wanted to be fixed. I had lost all hope what so ever that my life by society's definition would be normal. I tried reaching out to God, but I felt like He wasn't listening either. Instead, I just hid my true feelings, as always, to make it easier on those around me. I felt like a burden - something that was taking away the energy and time from everyone who was around me.

I was struggling on and off with suicidal thoughts, blaming myself and others, being mad at God. I would ask God questions like: What is my purpose? Why am I here? I felt I was wasting away and doing nothing with my life and I was wondering: Where are you, God? I would ask God: Can you help me? And I would feel like I was not receiving any answer. As a result, I started to turn away from my faith. I kept thinking that if I were patient enough, God would eventually repay me. Eventually, suicide seemed like a much quicker and easier answer to end my pain.

As I progressed into high school, the physical and emotional side of me said Let's get this over with and die. But the spiritual and mental side of me said: No, let's keep fighting. Even then, I believed that suicide is never a solution. I've never been one to give up and quit. What I wanted was a solution: To know what the reason was for me to live.

One thing that did keep helping me through all of this was my best friend Patrick. He's always been one of those friends that no matter what, he'd be there in a pinch. I have come to know and love him so much that if he needed a heart I would give him mine in a heart beat, because the world would be a little less special without a friend like Patrick.

Even though I was surrounded by people who loved me and cared about me, I still felt completely and utterly alone. So I ended up doing things the way I wanted to do, regardless of the consequences. That caused me to become somebody I did not like. As I progressed from age 14 to15, I began to not care about how I affected people. If I hurt your feelings, I didn't care. If I lied, or was manipulative, or used others for personal gain, I didn't care. I never showed to others how much I didn't care. I pretended I felt happy for other people. But inside, I didn't care about anything.

I didn't care what I was eating or drinking and didn't care if it was harming my body. I was in a cloud that surrounded me completely. There were people who tried to cheer me up by doing something nice, but it would piss me off instead. Even though I was polite, inside I'd say, "Screw you!" I didn't care anymore whether I lived or died or if I failed or succeeded at anything. I went to church now because my parents made me, not because I wanted to. I didn't believe in anything anymore. Things went on like this for me until the summer of 2005, when something unexpected changed my life forever.

Chapter 14

CRISIS

Days before my crash

Throughout 2004-2005, when I was 14 and 15, I began having unexplained "episodes" which became more and more frequent. The episodes included headaches and dizziness. I'd have something like deja vu and a heat flash all mixed together; it seemed to be some sort of out-of-body experience. At first, the doctors couldn't explain these episodes. I would feel it coming on and would let my family know that I was going away. I'd say, "I think I'm going somewhere." It was new and we didn't know how serious it really was. So we would all laugh and they would ask me, "Where are you going?"

Doctors ran tests on me to try to understand what the "episodes" were. I remember having a cap with electrodes on my head. The doctors said it wasn't a seizure because I could still talk when it was happening. They didn't know what was happening. I was losing weight, too. Nobody really noticed how much weight I lost because it was gradual, but looking back at photographs, you can see my arms and legs looked like sticks. And my ribs were sticking out as if I had almost no flesh on them.

My parents look back at those pictures now and they're shocked; shocked that neither my mom nor my dad saw how thin and drawn I looked. They'd bathed me and clothed me. But the slow weight loss had been going on for over a year. The episodes had been going on for about two years. No one thought they were related or a result of the muscular dystrophy.

The year that I turned 15, toward the end of school, I got the usual battery of tests before going to MDA camp. One was a lung-function test that I got at least every year, sometimes more often. Normally, we didn't hear anything back from the doctor after the lung-function test and we didn't that time, either. We thought nothing of it. But then,the day before I was due to leave for camp, the doctor's office called.

Somehow, the results of my test had been overlooked and they hadn't called right away. The news was grim. I was not getting enough oxygen. I was not exhaling enough, therefore retaining carbon dioxide in my system which causes carbon dioxide poisoning. The carbon dioxide poisoning was the cause of my episodes which were really seizures. This also explained why I was losing so much weight. The doctor informed us that he believed my body was having these "episodes" or seizures due to the high amount of carbon dioxide retained. On top of that great news, the doctor said it was not safe for me to attend camp, that I was one episode away from "never returning." He felt that the episodes would become more frequent because of my high carbon dioxide levels. With so many activities, camp would put me over the edge. My episodes were already daily. They were a normal part of my day-to-day activities. I had faced plenty of near-death experiences before in my life, so ignoring doctor's orders was not as unusual for me as you might think.

Besides, being from a very stubborn family, with that mulish independence flowing through my veins, I sometimes disregarded a doctor's recommendation. After all, doctors have been wrong pretty much my entire life. I take every thing doctors say with a massive grain of salt. I'd been told again and again I was going to die soon, so that was nothing new. I always said that I would rather die than to miss camp, and it was true. I wanted to take the risk. I was always pushing the limits of what I could do … especially when somebody told me I couldn't do it.

Of course my parents were scared to let me go. It was a week in the middle of nowhere with no hospitals around. But on the flip side, Mom knew how important it was to me. She often talked about the look of fulfillment and happiness on my face when I came home from my 'happy place'. I said to her that I would rather be dead than to miss camp. That's how I felt. My parents felt it was partly my decision – I was old enough to understand the risks. So I went to camp.

I pretty much just ignored my daily episodes, which didn't seem so bad. I was so resentful and careless about the diagnosis. I actually forgot about my risk. If I had an episode, I'd just tell myself, "F-U! Stop being weak; get over yourself!" I was so stubborn, I didn't even tell anybody. If I was having an episode; nobody knew.

When I arrived back home on Friday, I felt very tired but just attributed it to a great week. At camp, it was usual for us to be constantly on the go: fishing, arts and crafts, dances, not to mention staying up late each night playing cards. A lot of things were happening the weekend that I returned home. My older brother Alex was heading off to a Marine infantry school in North Carolina for 8 weeks, and my father was heading off for Thailand for a business meeting. That Saturday, after Dad left from the airport, the rest of us went out to dinner to see Alex off. My mom and younger brother Nathan and I left the restaurant to go back home and head to bed, as usual.

My mom lay me down on the bed to get my Pj's on. We talked about the events of the day as well as the fun things I remembered from camp. Mom turned around to grab my Pj's in the dresser. And that's all I remember.

Mom described what happened next: I was in Evin's dresser putting clothes away and getting his Pj's out to dress him for bed. We were laughing and joking and I asked Evin a question about camp…he didn't answer me…I asked again…. still no answer…I turned around a little annoyed at this point and said… Evin!… "Did you hear me"?

I turned around expecting Evin to be making some silly face, but what I saw terrified me to my core. Where I had just seen a lively boy talking so carefree about the exciting moments he shared at camp, I now saw my sons' eyes rolled back in his head, face blue, and tongue swollen. As I looked closer, his whole body was blue and he wasn't responding. It happened so fast! I was paralyzed for what seemed like an eternity. A great feeling of panic was flickering inside me and for a brief moment I couldn't move. He was dying before my eyes and I felt so helpless.

I have never felt so scared, so out of control before or since in my life.

SAVE HIM! That one thought pushed me to move with a sense of clarity and I dropped everything and ran over to him shouting his name over and over, "EVIN! EVIN! EVIN!" I shook him so hard just hoping for some response. My child's life was literally in my hands and all I could do was hope I was doing the right things to save him. I continued to yell....Evin, Evin....Still...no response! I ran as fast as I could into the living room grabbed the phone to dial 911 at the same time screaming for Nathan to come downstairs. I ran back to Evin's room! The operator was asking me what was my emergency and all I could get out, as I was running back to his room was, "my son's not breathing! My son's not breathing!"

Nathan finally ran down to Evin's room and panicked at the site of what he was seeing. Nathan was only 12 and I didn't want him in the house while all this was going on so I told him sternly to call his brother Alex with my cell phone, tell him what was going on and go outside and wait for the ambulance.

The 911 Operator said, "Ok, Listen to me"...She was trying to get more information out of me. I was so scared in that moment. I wasn't listening to a word she was saying, I thought to myself over and over...this isn't happening! This isn't happening! The operator was trying to calm me down. "Where is he?" He's on the bed, "Ok, Get him off the bed and lay him flat onto the floor." "You're going to do CPR."

I put the phone down and picked up my son to lay him on the floor. He was so heavy and limp in my arms, I didn't want to let him go. When I laid him down I suddenly realized he was not able to lie flat on his back. I picked up the phone frantic and tried explaining to the operator...I can't lay him flat. "What do you mean" she asked? I can't lay him flat! He's disabled! "Just try to lay him flat" she repeated as if not understanding the situation. I put the phone down and tried so hard to get his back flat on the floor but it just wasn't happening, I picked up the phone still panicked and I tried once again to tell the operator Evin still wasn't flat on his back. "OK, I think I understand but you need to do your best to get air into his lungs." The operator began to give me instructions for CPR. I was having difficulty holding the phone and trying to manipulate Evin's neck to start CPR.

Getting oxygen into Evin was no easy task. Evin's neck contractures are so bad his neck won't tilt back. This means it's difficult to get air into his lungs instead of his stomach. Because his body is twisted with Scoliosis and one of his lungs is compressed and almost non-functional, his heart wasn't positioned where it's supposed to be, and even a professional would have a tough time doing CPR on Evin. I Looked at his lifeless discolored body and was horrified by the thought that my son was dying before my eyes and everything the 911 operator was telling to do to save my sons life was impossible for me to do.

I had CPR training but in my panicked and emotional state I went completely blank. All I knew was I needed to get air into my son's lungs until the ambulance could get there, so I started mouth to mouth. As I breathed air into Evin time and time again, I could see a little color come back into his face. With each breath I felt a little sense of relief...so I kept breathing for Evin hoping and praying the paramedics would arrive soon. It seemed like an eternity.

By the time the paramedics arrived, some of Evin's color had returned. I have no idea how I was able to accomplish it, but I did and I'm so grateful I was somehow able to keep it together.

The paramedics went to work right away and I stepped back to give them room and to check on Nathan. The paramedics started an IV and intubated Evin right away and they were out the door faster than I could ask questions. One of my neighbors took care of Nathan and I jumped in the back of the ambulance with my purse and shoes in hand. The ride to the children's hospital downtown took about 20 minutes. Evin seemed to be stable for now so I reached into my purse to grab my phone which hardly had any juice so I quickly called as many people as I could think of: Alex, our preacher, Betty, family and a friend who worked with Scott because Scott was still on a plane to Thailand.

In the ER, after they stabilized Evin, the doctor wanted to do a tracheotomy right away. Evin was still unconscious. The doctors told me this is what they needed to do but I asked them to wait.

The news spread fast and the waiting room filled up while Evin was unconscious and in intensive care. People from MDA, church friends, neighbors and family all came when they heard the news to lend their support. Finally, Alex walked in the door and I was so relieved to see him. I could tell he was visibly shaken but having him there was so comforting. I needed him there, and he needed to be there as well.

Evin was stable for the moment so our preacher, Doug asked me if I wanted to go home to get an overnight bag so I could come back and stay the night. I was torn inside because I didn't want to leave Evin. What if he woke up and I wasn't there? What if something else happened and I wasn't there? I agonized over the decision but decided I would go if me and the preacher could go quickly so we left. We weren't gone 10 minutes when I got a call from the hospital saying Evin had another massive seizure and we immediately turned around and came right back. I didn't leave again!

When I returned, I was met with the doctors who were able to stabilize Evin once again and called me into a private room with our preacher and a few Elders from our church and said, Look! This is serious! If Evin has one more seizure, he might not survive. I broke down and cried for the first time feeling the weight of the world on my shoulders. I had just saved my son's life only to be faced with making a decision that could end it. I begged them to please wait until Evin's dad got back. A church friend who worked with Scott had gotten a message to him when he landed in Thailand and he was working on getting back home. The return trip would take almost two days and I begged them to just stabilize Evin. It was such a big decision. Before this time, we had conversations with Evin about someday needing to be on a ventilator but he had stated that he never wanted to be on a ventilator because everyone he knew who went on a vent had died or else they had little or no life.

The doctors told me if he didn't have the tracheotomy and use a ventilator machine, he would die. They said that Evin's carbon dioxide would increase and he would die quickly. I felt it was too huge of a decision to make alone. I begged them could they please just get Evin stable enough to survive until my husband returned? They said they would try."

Nathan Visiting at Hospital

Chapter 15

TO BANGKOK AND BACK

Dad made it back

When I left active duty in the military," says Dad, "we moved to Memphis, with the whole point was to be with the family more. To be there more for Melisa, and to help more with Evin. Even though I wasn't deploying overseas anymore for long periods, even the short business trips that I was taking for my new civilian health care job meant I was away and not there to help Melisa".

Evin recalls that his Dad was working for an orthopedics implant firm. At first helping to set up and run conferences and conventions, and then later after several promotions responsible for company international business which meant he had longer trips to do. When my respiratory failure happened, he was on his way to Bangkok.

Dad says: "Evin was getting really thin. We didn't know, of course, that it was due to his lack of oxygen, and the carbon dioxide poisoning. His body was atrophying and he was getting thinner and thinner. We just thought he didn't have any appetite. His attitude was positive and he didn't seem lethargic. He was excited about going to camp. However, tests showed he wasn't getting enough oxygen, so we said no to camp. But this was his one big thing each year …going to camp. Mentally, emotionally and psychologically, he lived for this. So we said to the doctor, if you give us an absolute no, he won't go. But if you give us a maybe, he's going to go. The doctor gave us a maybe and off he went to camp. He had a wonderful time."

"When I went to pick him up from camp, I noticed he was even thinner. And he was tired, very tired. He had always been tired after spending a week of fun and excitement and getting little sleep at camp. So we just assumed he needed some rest."

"I remember telling Melisa on that Saturday before I left for the airport that if he's not better by Monday, she really should take him to the doctor. Before I left for the airport, I sat down with Evin. Looking him in the eyes and said, 'You're 15 years old now son and you know your body better than anyone and should be able to tell us if something's wrong. If something is wrong, you need to tell your mom and she'll take you to the doctor.' Evin did not like going to the doctor. He thought they didn't know what they were doing."

After about 18 hours of travel, I landed in Bangkok. It was about five a.m. As I was walking up the jet way from the airplane to the terminal, there was a woman standing there in the middle of the jet way, which I've never seen before, with a sign. When I got closer to the sign I saw that it said, "Mr. Hartsell." I thought, that's odd; why would they do that? I thought it was a business related thing–may be they changed the hotel, the time of the meeting. I said, Hi, I'm Mr. Hartsell. "You're Mr. Hartsell?" Yes I said, and the woman said, "Please follow me." She took me into a private office and a more senior person from the airlines came in and said, "Sir, you need to call this phone number." It was a Memphis, Tennessee phone number. I asked, Why? And she said, "Sir, I can't tell you. You need to call this number." I thought, that's odd. It wasn't our home number. Again, I thought it was a business thing. It was a Memphis area code so I thought my job was calling me about a business related issue. Maybe they wanted me to say something different at the meeting."

"I dialed the number-knowing five a.m. in Thailand was late afternoon to early evening in Memphis. Jeff Wooden, a good friend and one of the elders of our church, answered the phone. It was his number I had been given. He said, 'Scott, this is Jeff Wooden. I've got some news and immediately I'm thinking, there's been a car wreck. Melisa's been hurt, seriously injured, or been killed? Are the boys OK? Alex was driving at this point; he was 18 years old. I said, "Jeff, what's wrong?" He paused and said, "Evin's in the hospital." I thought OK, so nobody was dead. That's good. Evin's being in the hospital wasn't the big shock I was dreading to hear. There could be any number of reasons he'd be in the hospital. I said, "OK." He said, "Melisa's there with him. You need to come home. I said, OK, what's wrong? What's happened? Again, Jeff was trying to be kind; to soften the blow and he said, "Evin's had an episode where he stopped breathing and they had to take him to the hospital. He's on ventilation right now, but you need to come home. Decisions need to be made." That hit me like a sledge hammer. Then my Marine, husband, and father instincts kicked in - I started thinking OK – what needs to be done? I immediately went back into the airport and went to the ticket counter. I had to wait though. It was five a.m. and they didn't open until seven a.m. As I waited, fear and worry started to overwhelm me. What in the world is going on? Is Evin still alive? Will I make it back in time? Is Melisa okay?"

"I couldn't get a hold of Melisa or the hospital–I didn't even know which hospital to contact. As soon as the ticket counter opened, I got a ticket back to Memphis. I then called my company and they said: 'Absolutely, we'll take care of it; whatever you need.' "They even had my ticket upgraded to first class. It seemed as though everyone was working to get me back home as quickly as possible."

"I stayed in the airport for four hours before my flight finally departed. It then took another day and a half to get home - basically three days from the time I had originally left Memphis. Just before I left Bangkok, I was finally able to get hold of Melisa. She described to me what had happened - how Evin had gone into respiratory failure, how he'd turned blue, and how Nathan had seen it all and had called for help. While she's telling me all of this, I'm bawling. I'm crying. Evin was in the best hospital in Memphis but all I could think about was Melisa being there alone and our son dying in her arms. That was really bothering me. I knew that if I had been there I couldn't have done anything more than she did. But my anguish was knowing that she had now experienced the horror of Evin almost dying in her arms, as I had when he was three years old. I knew what she was feeling and I had to get to her and Evin as soon as possible. That would still be 18 hours away."

Family Ready for Church

Chapter 16

EN ROUTE TO HEAVEN

Loving Mom

I was unconscious for three days, so, I don't know when it happened or how long it lasted. All I know is that it did happen. I remember a light…whether I was going to it or it was coming to me, I couldn' tell, but it just kept getting brighter and brighter. This wasn't your average type of light. It had a warm, comforting feel to it. Almost like this light was alive, holding me, protecting me. Before I knew what was going on, I found myself in a place I've never seen before. I saw pillars as high as the eye could see. I saw bright figures all around me. I could make out beings, but they didn't have physical bodies. What I believe I saw were spirits; but these spirits actually had different appearances. Similar to the way our bodies have different physical qualities, these "spirits" had unique qualities that made them look different from one another. Yet I can't describe how the difference appeared. It was just there.

More than anything else, I remember the emotions, the feelings I had in that place. The word that best describes what I was feeling is "tranquility." I had no fear. Fear did not even exist for me. Even if I had wanted to have fear, the ability to fear had been taken away. I felt serene and did not worry whether it was life, death, loss or gain. It was a feeling beyond peace. There was a rightness about it. It felt natural, like this was where I was supposed to be. I was so happy I wanted to cry, but I could not be sad in such a wonderful place.

I understand why people say they see a white light, but I prefer, "shining light." We live in a world with darkness, but no matter where I looked, darkness could not be found. There is no word that can describe the depth of love and compassion I felt from those spirits around me in that place. There is nothing, even to this day, that I can compare to what I experienced in that place.

Just as I started to truly understand where I was, as I stood there in this miraculous place, I began to feel myself being pulled, not really falling, but pulled back toward my body on earth. The next thing I knew, I was waking up in the hospital, not knowing what had happened, whether I was dead or alive. I remember thinking, "What's happening? Is this heaven? If this is heaven, I've been ripped off!" A tube was down my throat and for a moment I thought I was dead. It was not registering that I was in the hospital. I thought it might be heaven because of what I'd just experienced, but the bright lights of the hospital were not comforting like the shining light that I'd just experienced. I hadn't fully transitioned back to consciousness. It felt as though my body was on auto pilot. I couldn't talk because of the tube. My mind was racing. You prepare yourself in life for so many different things, but experiencing near-death and being resuscitated is not one of them.

When I heard what had actually happened, I was in shock and awe. I'd never come so close to death before. In an instant, I had gone from feeling fine to turning blue and dying. My heart had stopped. I had died and been resuscitated. At first, I wondered if people were exaggerating. In my mind, I went through every possibility: I knew my death experience wasn't a dream but maybe I was dreaming about the hospital. Maybe I was in a coma. Or maybe I was dead and this was all part of the death experience.

But eventually, I started to come back to reality. And the reality was this: I almost died from respiratory failure and I saw a bit of what I believe to be the afterlife. I didn't know what it meant, or why I experienced it. Did I experience it for a reason? Did I experience it because I was supposed to die and my mom brought me back? Truly, I'll never know why, but it definitely changed my life for the better. It was a gift from God. Without this experience, I wouldn't be where I am today.

Does that mean my depression was gone? No. In fact, the worst was yet to come. But this spiritual experience was a stepping stone for me. As I awoke, I felt just as I did as a child: Happy! I knew there was a heaven. Without doubt, I knew there was an afterlife, there was a God and He loved me.

Unfortunately, depression returned with a vengeance. Maybe I just chalked my "heaven" experience up to a dream. Maybe I no longer believed. Maybe I just got bitter all over again. Mostly, I just didn't think about it. I was in for more bad times, and the memory of this incredible experience didn't hit me with full force until years later.

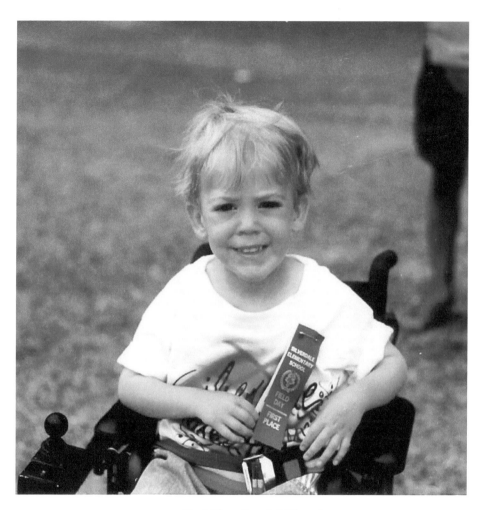

First Place Special Olympics

Chapter 17

CHANGED FOREVER

Miss Betty and Miss Hope

While I was unconscious for those three days, my mom stayed by my bedside day and night. Alex came as well but Mom convinced him to go on to his Marine training. Only when Miss Betty was there with me did my mother finally make it home to shower and change into clean clothes. Mom was afraid I'd wake up with that tube in my throat, unable to speak, and I'd freakout. My dad returned from Thailand shortly after I woke up, three days after the respiratory failure. We all had to make a decision. The doctors said I had to have a tracheotomy and a ventilator machine. I didn't want it. I was already dependent enough, and didn't want to be dependent on another machine.

Since I couldn't speak, my parents made me an A-Z alphabet on paper and gave me a long straw so I could point to letters. This revealed that I was a pathetic speller. Until then, even I didn't know how bad a speller I was. At least our spelling-talks gave us a lot of laughs. This whole time, my room in the ICU was packed. I'm not going to lie: All the attention I got was pretty nice, though I hated that I was putting my parents through this whole ordeal. My church elders and the preacher were there by my bedside, followed by a barrage of family and friends. The biggest surprise in all of this was the support from the workers, volunteers and campers from MDA camp. Every day the room, as well as the hallways up and down the hospital, was packed. It was overwhelming to experience the love and support of so many people.

The trache decision was hard. My parents had to decide how much of it would be their decision and how much would be mine. I was old enough to understand the situation and the risks. But then the doctors gave us another option, and I wanted to try it: A BiPAP machine. The BiPAP machine is similar to the CPAP machine, which people use for sleep apnea. The BiPAP machine has a mask that you put over your nose and mouth at night, and it provides air pressure to force air into your lungs as you sleep. However, the BiPAP, unlike the CPAP, is not continuous air pressure. The machine forces you to breathe in and then takes the pressure off so you can breathe out. We decided to try the BiPAP option and the doctors took the tube out of my throat.Again, I was breathing completely on my own.

The next several weeks we spent in what was called the hospital's "Transitional Unit." Every night, I slept with the BiPAP machine. There was a small cot in my hospital room, and my Mom and Dad were always with me. One night my dad would sleep there, the next night it would be my mom. The nurses couldn't believe that my parents were there every day and night. There were kids, even babies, that no one came to see. I know it was stressful and exhausting for my parents. They were both working at the time. But they always showed up. They were afraid I'd have another seizure, another sudden respiratory failure. I didn't like the BiPAP. The mask was uncomfortable and chafed me. While I had the ability to breathe in and out; I just couldn't breathe hard enough. The machine gave me air,but only when it wanted to give me air, which made me feel as though I had no control over my breathing. In the end, I didn't have a choice. After all that effort, the BiPAP didn't work. I still wasn't getting enough oxygen in my blood. That left only one option: full tracheotomy and a ventilator machine.

To understand the struggle I was facing, you have to understand my experience of tracheostomies. Every one of my friends or campers with MD who had this procedure passed away soon after having it. So, my options seemed to be don't have the procedure, die; or, have the procedure, die. Hmmm, this would be a toughfy. As I was wrestling with the consequences of such a decision, the doctor gave me yet another bit of "wonderful" news! He said, "This procedure has a possibility of irrevocably altering your voice. You may never be able to eat by mouth, talk, or sing again." This was terrible. Using my voice was very,

very important to me. My throat was pretty much the only muscle I still had and it helped me communicate with the world. My voice was all I really had to connect me with other people. As far as not being able to sing was concerned, that was almost worse. Singing was one thing that really brought me joy. Every one of us is given certain talents or abilities in life. The one thing I felt I had was special was singing. I was blessed with a good voice and I enjoyed performing in the choir.

But if I didn't have the tracheotomy, I would surely die. My weight had dropped to only 60 pounds and I was almost dying from carbon dioxide poisoning. I had no real choice. With the support of both my parents, I decided to have the procedure that would forever change the way I lived.

I remember the doctor's words very clearly. When he told me I would never be able to sing again, I responded, "Oh yeah, watch me. I'll come back and show you!" After surgery, I found out that while I was under, my parents had the doctors do another muscle biopsy. This is when we discovered that my form of MD is merosin deficiency and seizures can be part of this disease. The high carbon dioxide was making that worse. The doctors told us that merosin deficiency MD is so rare that I may be the oldest and possibly one of the first with my severity of merosin deficiency. At the time of my birth, the doctors said, there were only 15 known people with my type of MD in the world. So I felt just a little scared that I had no one to ask about what to expect. It became more frustrating because now I wasn't exiled just by being disabled but also by the type and rarity of my disability.

When I awoke from surgery, having an extra hole in my throat felt very weird, very strange. I was told the surgery went well; I woke up and I realized I couldn't speak. I panicked. But the doctors said that I couldn't speak because my "cuff" was inflated. I didn't know what a cuff was. As it turns out, it's a little balloon attached to the trach inside my throat which can be filled with water or air. The cuff prevents fluids from the mouth from draining into the lungs while sleeping. It also prevents the air from escaping upward through my mouth instead going downward to inflate my lungs.

Two days later, they deflated the cuff and I was able to talk, even though my throat was extremely sore. I started eating easy foods, like mashed potatoes. We discovered my swallowing reflex had not been damaged, so I was able to eat by mouth. Yay! Also it dropped the pitch of my singing voice and raised the pitch of my speaking voice; having an extra hole in your throat makes you sound like a ten-year-old girl. My singing voice dropped down an octave … I used to be a tenor but it now really hurt to try to hit the high notes. I became a bass. I was just grateful to be able to sing.

Not too long after I had the trach operation, Alex came home from his military training and came to visit me. Here's what he remembers from this crisis event that changed my life:

ALEX HARTSELL

"Evin has this uncanny ability to make or break tension. He seems to do it so effortlessly. He can play with the moment like a cat batting a toy around. He's a great observer of people; he knows where and when he can do it."

"When Nate called me because Evin had respiratory failure, it was very scary. They were already on the way to the hospital. I was getting ready to leave for training the next morning. Nate was terrified, almost crying. He said Evin wasn't breathing; Nate thought he was dead. I said I was coming home but they told me to meet them at the hospital." "Evin was sprawled out on the bed and a few elders from our church congregation were there. Mom was there. Dad was still on his way to Asia. When I saw Evin, I was very disconcerted; I didn't know if he was alive or dead. It was a tunnel-vision moment. There were doctors all around. Finally, I could tell he was breathing, but we didn't know if he was going to make it. I didn' t know what to do; the doctors didn't even know what was wrong with him."

"I ended up leaving. I told Mom to contact me but I was in training and didn't know how things were progressing. Finally, Dad called the Colonel in charge of the base where I was training. They had served together in Iraq so the Colonel personally came to tell me that Evin was going to have the trach surgery."

"That week was very hard. I still didn't know what was happening. It made me realize how fragile Evin was, not just physically, but emotionally. He's experienced so much. I finally got to the hospital after the trach operation and I was really anxious. I was just getting back from Marine Corps training and the whole family was waiting for me in the waiting area. I didn't know what

116

to expect. I went into Evin's room and I saw the hose in his throat. I don't know, maybe I went pale or something, and I said, "Okay, how does it feel? So Evin started whispering in this raspy voice, and I had to lean in close. He was whispering, "Oh it hurts so much, I can't talk, I can't talk anymore. I felt terrible and I said, "Evin, I'm so sorry…" Then he said in a normal voice, "Nah, I'm just kidding. It's totally okay." We were laughing. It was such a relief. I'll never forget that moment."

"He was always doing things like that. Another time, when we were younger and we were all at dinner at home, Nathan said something so ignorant, it was shocking. At that time, I used to help take care of Evin. In Romans 15:1, it says: *'Those who have strength are to bear the weaknesses of those without strength and not to please themselves.'* That was a part of who I was. I would take him to the bathroom, pick him up, dress him, feed him—he was comfortable with me doing all that."

"So I was sitting next to Evin preparing to feed him. It was so impactful, what Nathan said, it took us all aback and we sat there in this awkward silence. Evin whispered to me to lift his elbow, which I did often when he needed to scratch his face. I lifted his elbow and Evin slapped himself in the face and said, "Oh, Nathan, that is just so stupid." Everybody laughed. That was typical Evin."

"Evin has been through so much. He never got to do the growing-up things like dating, or being on his own. He's missed a huge part of the maturing process. But I do think he has a great attitude, especially considering all the things he's endured."

"Even though I grew up with Evin, it's hard for me to truly understand what he faces. I'm his brother. I saw him an hour after he was born, and I've seen him growing up. Sometimes the things he tells me are still difficult for me. His challenges are so overwhelming. He'll say, "Alex, you know what? I never get time alone … they're always there at all times." He'll say, "Alex, if I want to scratch my butt, somebody's gotta do it for me."

"He impresses me. He wants to be independent. He won't allow the world to crush him; he wants to grow and to go out on his own. That's what inspires me about Evin. He continues to grow, to struggle."

16th Birthday Party

Chapter 18

VENTILATOR BLUES

Getting Used to Ventilator

After the surgery, I kept worrying and wondering, "What now?" I was already disabled and in a wheelchair, and now I was also on a ventilator. If my life was hard before and I had no hope of ever excelling at anything, I now thought there was nothing I could do. How many people do you see out in public with a trach? I don't see many. They are not living what society defines as a "normal" life. I felt it was another nail in my coffin. It was like: Come on! Seriously? It was overwhelming having to deal with another major issue. It was a huge change. I knew I had to do it, but I really wasn't prepared.

When I first awakened from my near-death experience, I was filled with peace and joy. But once I went home dragging a ventilator around in addition to the wheelchair, those feelings were all gone. The depression was back. I knew nothing of heaven. All that was left was my new reality.

Being on a ventilator was hard. It was scary, unpredictable and frustrating. There were so many things I had to learn … or suffer massive consequences.

Unlike many patients, I wasn't completely dependent on the vent machine: I could breathe through the tube in my neck without it. I controlled when I took a breath, and the machine just helped. But so many things could go wrong with the equipment the tube could crimp, cutting off the air, or it could damage my throat – For example, if the tubing caught on somebody or something going by, it would damage the inside of my throat. Maybe fluid from the humidifier could build up, travel up the tube into my lungs and drown me…and soon. Any one of these things could kill me. For the first two weeks at home, we had 24-hour nurses who continued to train my parents.

Many people are not aware that seriously disabled children often get very little medically-necessary nursing care at home. If a parent works, they are likely to have too much money to qualify for extra help and too little to afford private nursing. A disabled child like me was eligible for only 8 hours a week nursing care at home. Once I turned 18 and was an official adult, I would qualify for more. But until then, my parents had to take care of everything. So, after the two weeks of supervision and training my parents at home, the nurses cut their hours back until we were left with only eight hours a week.

Physically, I felt much better after the trach operation–I had much more energy and my appetite came back – but my entire reality was crumbling. I couldn't go anywhere by myself any more. The trach separated me even more from the other kids. I'd always been an out going person who talked to everyone and wasn't afraid to try new things. Now, all that changed.

I started to become a recluse, staying at home all the time, not going out with anybody. I withdrew. For the first time, my parents really saw a personality change in me. I was moody and unhappy all of the time and no longer interacted with others. My mother didn't know what to do. She says she was always guessing. It's hard enough to raise an adolescent who is healthy, but raising one with a disability? She tried to make our lives as normal as possible. My younger brother Nathan starting having trouble of his own. He was being bullied at school. My parents tried changing schools for him. In fact, my senior year in high school, we moved to another district just so he could be in a better school. My mother drove me to school every day so that I could finish my senior year at my old high school. By that time she had begun to work in real estate. So she drove me to school, went to work, picked me up and took me home. Twice a week, a nurse came for the afternoon, so Mom could go back to work on those days. People have always tended to say I'm an inspiration, but in truth, my mother is the real inspiration. How she managed it all without help is amazing.

My Parents tried hard to get more nursing hours. They made endless phone calls. Finally, the state of Tennessee put my name on a list to get additional services. I was number 800 on the list. Social Services suggested that my mother should quit her job and be my full-time nurse. Or that she should go back to school and become a licensed nurse. Since it would probably take more than five years for my name to come up, Social Services also suggested that my parents get a divorce. That way, Mom and I would qualify for more help. Some parents, they said, choose that option. I'm not sure if Mom was very polite to the people who made this suggestion. My parents did not choose this option.

Brotherly Support

Chapter 19

NURSE KICK-ASS

My Nurses

A Month shy of my 18th birthday, just after I graduated from high school, my father got a job offer in Florida. The new job as a hospital administrator meant that even though he'd have to work long hours, he'd be able to be at home much more and travel far less. He decided to take it. I think another reason he accepted the offer had to do with the nursing laws. At 18, I would be eligible for 24-hour nursing under our insurance. But the nursing laws in Tennessee did not allow nurses to drive their patients, or do much of anything besides take care of them in the home. That meant I would still be bound by the walls of home, not able to have my own life. The nurses in Florida could drive me anywhere, any time. They could help me live a truly independent life. We packed up, sold the house and moved all in a matter of weeks. One week later, I turned 18 and my mother helped me apply for the 24-hour nursing care. In this case, my ventilator created an opportunity for me having a vent makes it necessary to have 24-hour nursing care. Only with 24-hour care and mobility could I ever hope to have independence.

By this time, my personality had devolved. The nice, caring, loving, sweet person I once was had disappeared. I was very rude, impatient, and immature. It took many years for me to realize that my legs may be disabled but my manners were not. I had to painfully catch up, step by step, in order to become an acceptable human being by society's standards.

All the way through high school, no one ever discussed what would come next for me. There was nothing about branching out. My parents expected me to go to college, but to me it seemed like a useless exercise. I felt like I was in the way using up resources… money, space, time and the efforts of others to help me, when it. I knew that it was all going to amount to nothing. Now that high school was over, I was sure that there was no company in the world that would hire me. I had turned 18 years old with an 8-year-old's mind-set. Even though my parents had tried to teach me to be as independent as possible, I never scheduled my own appointments, went grocery shopping for myself, or even ordered my own food at a restaurant. At this age, you should already know how to do laundry, keep a schedule, and take care of your own hygiene. If it weren't for someone brushing my teeth, I wouldn't do it. I felt like a baby must feel when waiting for someone to take care of it, without the ability to make decisions.

I had been "inspiring" my whole life and knew I would hear about it for the rest of my life. But I didn't want to be a hero just for waking up and getting my clothes on, for just living. I wanted to be good at other things…something that could actually affect the world on a larger scale, more than just meeting people for a moment and making them feel motivated. I began to think no one wanted me around because no one ever asked me "Hey, can you help me with this or hey, you want to go and hang out?" I believed that I truly was wasting resources by just living. I would get so angry and disrespectful sometimes. I just didn't care about anything. I would say anything,whether it was rude, insulting, or hurtful. In my mind and heart, I thought: This is how life is for a disabled person. I just have to accept it. Life is just crap! I felt like I had nothing to do for the next 60 plus years, except to wait for death.

This was my mindset as we began our new lives in Florida. As soon as we arrived, my parents enrolled me in a small, local Christian college. I was so passive, I didn't tell them, I didn't want to go. It never even occurred to me to refuse! A week later, when I turned 18, we applied for disability and full-time nursing. It would take weeks before we were actually able to get a nurse, so three times a week, my mother drove me to school, hung around campus reading or doing something else till I was finished, and then we'd drive home. I hated it.

I am a very spiritual person but at this Christian college, I didn't feel an abundance of Godly love from my professors and peers. I felt like I was in a Stepford Wives movie. Everybody just did what they were told as if brainwashed, and so did I. It was boring. There was required religious studies instruction, and there were no opinions or ideas or thinking outside the box. Eventually I switched to the local community college.

Meanwhile, once we got approval to hire nurses, we had to find a home health nursing agency that accepted our insurance. We didn't know it at the time, but the agency itself that supplies nurses is almost as important as the nurses themselves. Agencies create the rules for the nurses and can make it easy or hard to live life. The first agency we found was a large nationally recognized nursing agency. I felt very entitled during this time. I expected that everything I wanted would be done immediately. So when it came to finding nurses, it was hard. Because it's not just about whether or not they can take care of you; it's also about whether or not they can stand you.

One of my first male nurses was a young white man with short hair and an average build named Alex. He was maybe in his 20s. He seemed very willing but he wasn't very good at dealing with a rude, entitled and impatient client. I don't think we lasted half a day. I expected him to jump when I asked for something, and he seemed pretty slow. Finally, he got so frustrated that he shouted, "KISS MY ASS!" My mom was about to run in from her side of the house, but my dad caught her arm. He wanted to see how I'd handle it before they had to intervene. They heard me shout back, "Get the hell out of my house. You're fired!" It was the first time I'd ever stood up for myself. My parents were proud!

There were other trials and missteps. One nurse didn't stay at my house for more than a day. Larry came that day for orientation. It looked as though he weighed at least 400 pounds. He was very nice, very kind, but when we got to the point where we were teaching him how to transfer me from the chair to the bed, I became doubtful. I have a lift people can use, or they can just pick me up. Larry said he could pick me up. My first thoughts were (trying not to be rude or mean) you can barely pick yourself up; how can you pick me up? But I didn't say it aloud; I didn't want to be hurtful. So I said, "Go for it!" I was about 90 pounds then. Larry picked me up, getting a good hold on me. He placed his left arm under my knees and the other behind my back under my right armpit. Then he had to turn left to start going from the chair towards the bed.

Holding me up, he started to walk towards the bed when he realized, halfway there, he couldn't make it and was about to drop me. Instead of asking for help from the other nurse standing by, he tried to toss me on to the bed. The problem was he didn't throw me high enough. So I went flying into the metal side of the bed. I bounced off it and landed on the floor. Larry, who was already falling from trying to throw me, fell and landed on top of me … with all the weight of his 400 pounds. You know how sometimes when you're hurt and you want to scream but you're just going uhhhh, uhhhh … what happened? It was like that. The other nurse helped him get up and off of me. Then she helped me get up and lifted me up onto the bed. Luckily, I wasn't hurt. I am pretty used to being crushed, hurled, thrown and just falling. So it wasn't too bad. But that was the end of Larry.

A few of the nurses had a problem with me as a normally sexual person. One time a female nurse saw that I had woken up with an erection and she said to my mother, "I didn't know he could do that!" She quit. Another nurse saw me masturbating. My mother told her it was normal. She quit. Another nurse had a drug problem. He was shaking so much, he couldn't feed me. Lunch involved some sushi flying past my face and smacking against the wall. He got fired. One nurse was sweet. She was in her mid-to-late-70s, but still very active … go, go, go. But within the first five minutes of her day, as soon as I told her I was going to college, she started crying. "You're so brave, you're so brave," she sobbed. I thought: All right, you're so emotional over this, what are you going to do when something bad happens? I just smiled and we got through the four-hour teaching process. She left and I called the nursing agency and told them, "She's not coming back!"

Finally, a young woman with two young daughters came to work at my house: Jennifer. She and I connected almost immediately. Jennifer was pivotal for me. She had a strong personality; she didn't take much crap and she knew how to deal with an impatient, smart-aleky child. She was motherly but also a friend. She really understood how to help me grow up.

She would push me to leave the house when I would rather stay at home and play video games; I wanted to stay in my comfort zone instead of exploring outside life. Jennifer would encourage me to try more things. I had never gone to a restaurant without my parents or a relative. Jennifer got me to go out to the Cracker Barrel restaurant one day. We were sitting at the table with the waiter, waiting to order. Jennifer ordered first. Then she looked at me for me to give my order. Believe it or not, even though I was18 years old, I had never ordered for myself at this point. I would tell my parents what I wanted and they would order for me. I quietly told Jennifer what I wanted. But she didn't say any thing. I kept staring at her for her to tell the waiter what I wanted, like my parents did for me. Jennifer looked back at the waiter and said, "I guess he doesn't want any thing," and handed him the menus back. The waiter walked away.

I just sat there. This had never happened to me before. I had never experienced anyone as blunt and brassy as Jennifer before. I wasn't confrontational. I didn't know what to do. Jennifer's food came, minutes passed and I still had not gotten the courage to order my food. I watched her eat for about 10 more minutes before finally breaking out of my comfort zone and trying something new. I called the waiter over and asked for my own food for the first time in 18 years. Jennifer was treating me like the equal individual that I was and not like a person in a wheelchair who needs help with every single little thing. I clearly had a lot of catching up to do. There are many different ways to get a person to face their fears. This was a very direct way of doing it. It may not work for everyone, but it worked for me.

Parents might want to push their disabled child, but the question is - how hard? What are the boundaries for someone like me? It was hard to tell; it was all trial and error. At first I thought that Jennifer was just mean. After all, who would let a patient go without food, right? But looking back, now I know that it was my first step toward growth and independence.

Jennifer's daughters opened up to me very quickly. Normally kids will stare at some body like me; they don't know what to say or how to act. They try to figure out if I'm man or machine. I'm guessing because their mom is a nurse, they didn't see me as abnormal. Sally who was five, and Patricia who was seven, were amazing and I loved them very much. They were very funny and quite protective of me. The first time I went out with them, we went to the mall. Somebody was staring at me and Sally got up on a table and yelled, "What are you looking at!" That's what they were like. I was obsessed with everyone's opinion of me. If I wasn't being rude, I was being a doormat - eager to please everyone around me. My parents had protected me from anyone who might exploit me, and I'd never experienced anyone who acted really selfishly. So I didn't realize there was a darker side to Jennifer; I was always compliant. Jennifer was very bossy and eventually, she started to manipulate me. At first, she seemed to be just a wonderful person; but after a while, another side emerged.

Since I was allowed only eight hours of nursing a day, I was limited to one nurse, and it was Jennifer. When my hours were expanded to 16, Kathy was hired. It was after Kathy came on board that the trouble started to brew. I liked Kathy right away but I didn't feel joined at the hip like I did with Jennifer. Kathy was blunt, honest, and could teach a sailor how to curse. She taught me how to think for myself, make my own decisions, and be assertive. That didn't go down so well with Jennifer. Slowly, tension began to build. After many months, maybe almost a year, the tension got heated. It eventually exploded into war.

My Caregivers

Chapter 20

THE NURSE WARS

Memphis Trip

The first day we met it was three weeks past my 19th birthday. My mother and another nurse, Jennifer, were taking care of me at the time. Jennifer had the morning shift and Kathy wanted me for the evening shift, 3 to 11 p.m. At that time, I could get only 16 hours of nursing a day. Jennifer felt I was very polite. I wanted to engage in conversation. I was interested in learning about her and what she liked."

My nurse, Kathy, had dark hair that fell across her face and she pushed it back carelessly with stained fingers. She was middle-aged and looked tired at times. She could tell I was fishing for her interests, like I wanted to be able to entertain her and keep her happy. She had a husky voice and her gravelly laughter gurgled up from way inside.

I said I always tried to be extremely polite for orientation because I never knew how the nurse would be. I wanted to put on a good face, just in case. Then as I got more relaxed, my true manners would emerge. When she first started working with me, I was a bit immature and very self-centered. I wasn't good at expressing my needs. I had no patience and desperately wanted to be first. I felt that when I said jump, she was supposed to say 'how high?' When I wanted something, I wanted it right then and there. She realized I was being spoiled; it was time to open my eyes. So, when I said I wanted something, she'd say, 'Wait a minute,' and I'd get mad. Then we'd start fussing at each other. She said, 'Just because you're in a wheelchair doesn't mean you're entitled to priority. You can wait just like everybody else. You're not going to die; it's not life-threatening. I'm in the middle of doing something ... you have to learn patience.'

Here's what Kathy recalls of that time; "You were not accustomed to socializing with people outside of your circle. You needed to be exposed to other people and to the ways of the world. You needed to see that there was more to life than your little circle of friends, family and church folks."

"It was hard for you to grow up. Every other kid could slam their door or stamp their foot. You can't do those things; but you wanted to be accepted."

"I remember a particular incident; it will never leave my mind. You were trying to assert yout independence with your parents. You were trying to convey your feelings. You had broken some house rule, about your bedtime, I think."

"Your dad was very controlling. Your dad would cut off the home's Internet if he didn't like what Evin was looking at on the computer. I think they caught him looking at inappropriate internet sites one time. He'd follow your checking account and watch how you spent your money. You felt like every little detail of your life was controlled. Your father scolded you over this one thing as if you were a little child. It may have been your 10:30 bedtime. So you confronted your dad because you were an adult. But your father didn't budge. Your dad could be very stubborn; if he thought he was right, he wouldn't budge. When you came back into the room, you were sobbing-just sobbing. You were a 'basket case'. I had to console you and clean you up. I was so angry that your parents made you feel that way. You started talking about suicide. You didn't feel validated; they didn't understand what you were trying to say. They are very religious and you didn't feel that you could be open and honest with them. I'd say to you, 'Don't you know that they love you unconditionally? There's nothing in this world you can't say to your dad.' And you said, 'No, you're wrong.' Then I said, 'When he comes in the door that uniform comes off.' You replied, 'No, it doesn't.

I told Melisa that you was seriously talking about suicide. After that, your mom and dad had a discussion. Your mom realized they were still treating you like a child and they needed to let you grow. I think after that they sought medical help for your emotional and mental state."

"Getting you out of your man-cave, your 'bat-cave' as we called it at the time, that little room where you were playing video games all the time – you needed to see there was more to the world than video games and church and your family. It was a fight; sometimes it's still a fight."

"I wanted to take you trick or treating and you said, 'I'm too old.' I responded, 'B.S. Let's go. It's Halloween,' and you said 'Are you serious?' I said, 'Yes, I'll ring doorbells.' Then you said, 'I don't have costume,' and I offered, 'Yes you do you're a handicapped kid.' You replied, 'You're crazy Kathy.' I think you were 19 or 20 when we did that. Still today, if I work with you on Halloween, I drag you out!"

"I took you to your first monster truck event. Some girl got drunk, got into a fight with you. You were holding your own! She said she was going to punch you. I'm thinking: 'I'm going to pound you if you try touch him. The girl kept telling you she wanted to sit down in your wheelchair because there were no chairs. You tried to explain to her you couldn't get out of your wheelchair, but she was too drunk to understand. She kept yelling that you were rude and not a gentleman; she cursed you out. Then she made a weird face. You backed up and she projectile vomited. After that, they moved."

"One time when I was getting ready for a date, you insisted on going shopping with me. I hadn't had a date in years. You were trying to dress me … encouraging me to have a social life. 'Nope that doesn't look good on you; take it off.' Needless to say, the guy never showed up. You were pissed! 'I did all that work and he doesn't show up? You said 'tell me who he is I'll beat him up; I'll run him over with my chair.' This made me laugh so hard I coughed."

"When I first started working for you, I was guided by Jennifer about what you could do or not do. But after about a year, or maybe less, we got close. You started hinting at stuff. Something was going on behind the scenes, but I couldn't tell what. Then your behavior changed. The kid I used to greet when I came to work was disappearing. You seemed to be in turmoil. I didn't know where it was coming from – an outside source? From me? From your family?"

"One day I came into work and you were totally out of it. Emotionally, you were a wreck. But you wouldn't talk to me or tell me what was wrong. I told you if you were going to keep behaving like that, I'd have to leave. You told me I was doing this and that … I said, 'I'm not doing any of that. Where do you get your information from?' But you wouldn't talk to me. 'If you don't talk to me, I can't help you.' "You started crying. I'm thinking, 'Oh my God, what's wrong with this kid?' You said, 'I don't know what to do or say…' and you engulfed yourself in your game. You just ignored me. If I did interact with you, you would fight me."

"This stalemate went on for weeks. I treated you like you were my son – I have a son your age. And sometimes you have to fight with them to make them open their mouths. So, I pissed you off." "That's when you started spilling the beans about what the other nurse was telling you. You told me that Jennifer was complaining to you about me, telling you that I wasn't doing my job properly and that you should fire me. Sometimes she would threaten to quit and you felt afraid to lose her. You were very dependent on Jennifer. She was like a surrogate mother. It was deeply stressful and troubling to you and you didn't know how to handle it."

"But Jennifer was taking advantage of you in ways you didn't understand. When you enrolled in a new community college, instead of going to class with you, Jennifer enrolled in her own classes. She dropped you off in your class and went off to her own class. She almost lost her license over that. Jennifer would do a lot of shopping and errands for herself and her children on your time. When you got home and I asked what you'd bought, it was all stuff for Jennifer or for her girls, of whom you were very fond. Your parents said it was your money, and you could spend it however you wanted, but I thought you were being manipulated. Sometimes you would lie to your mother about how you spent your money on. And often, when they got home, none of the nursing chores would be done. No shower, no meds, no medical supplies, laundry, or cleaning. Sometimes, you had not even eaten all day. I thought it was abusive, I confronted Jennifer and told your parents about it. Right around this time, you qualified for a 24-hour nurse service. That's when Lois came on board."

"I describe Lois as dedicated, bossy, aggressive dominating nurse who was amazing. She had blonde hair, big glasses and a generous mouth; you could always hear her from far away. She was so high energy and so efficient, she seemed to do the work of four nurses at once. Her husband was disabled and needed full care, so when she left the Hartsell's house, she would go home to take care of him. Lois was definitely "all work and no play," but she was an excellent nurse. I figured things would settle down with a third nurse to come between Jennifer and me, but Jennifer managed to pit Lois against me."

"Your mother was getting more and more stressed. Jennifer complained to Melisa, Lois and you about me. I would take her concerns to Melisa and confront Jennifer. There was constant soap-opera drama in the house. The nurses could go home and leave it behind, but Melisa felt subjected to it 24-7. She was stressed and exhausted."

"I was still trying to figure out exactly what was going on. You would tell me, 'Jennifer said I had to go shopping with her before we could do my shopping,' or 'Jennifer said I should buy this.' And I asked you, 'How do you feel about that?' You said, 'What do you mean?' I said, 'Don't you know what those words mean? How do you feel about doing this or that?' You said, 'Nobody ever asked me that before. That's when I realized that you really didn't know how you felt about things. You'd say, 'Well, I feel this way, but I'm not sure. I don't know if that's how I'm supposed to feel. You thought your feelings were wrong unless somebody validated them. I would push you to get in touch with your feelings. I told you, 'Listen, son, you've got patient rights. Don't you know that?' Well apparently you didn't. So, I got you a book and I said, 'Read it, read it, read it. Knowledge is power. The more educated you are, the less other people can manipulate you."

"When I told you that my job role was the same as all the other nurses I saw the light bulb go on. The apron strings were getting cut. I told you to grow up. You have choices. When I took you shopping, I'd make you pick your own clothes. I'd make you choose … this soda or that soda, which one? Either pick or you're not going to get anything. When we were going to watch a movie, I would make you choose. Choose one, or watch nothing. You started to realize you had a brain; you weren't connected to everyone else. It was a whole new world to you."

"I recall a particular crisis that occurred over shopping at GameStop the computer-game store. It was a turning point for you. The more you did, the more I praised you. The more I praised you, the angrier Jennifer got."

"You wanted to go to GameStop and pick up a game and Jennifer wanted to do her shopping instead. She didn't want to take you to GameStop. But you said if you couldn't go to GameStop, she couldn't do her shopping. Through that experience, you learned, you had a choice. You could make a choice; you could make demands; you had a choice about your care."

"I think that was a big turning point with you. You had never talked back to Jennifer before. You were so proud of yourself. It was like a weight was lifted off of you. Jennifer was twisted about it; she never saw you behave like that before. You'd never said no to her before. I didn't know I had such a big impact on you until you told me that I had. I just do what I do. Sometimes, I don't realize what it means. But, according to you, I was breaking Jennifer's hold on you and Jennifer didn't like it. Both Jennifer and Lois demanded that you fire me. They said they'd both quit if you didn't and so you fired me."

"After I got fired I was gone for a year or maybe 14 months and I got a voicemail message from your mom. She said, 'Hey Kathy this is Melisa. Just wondering how you're doing. Evin misses you and we're wondering if you'd stop by for a visit. I went to visit on a Saturday. It was in April. I got to the house and there's a new nurse, Shawn, and your mom was in the TV room talking. I figure that I'd visit a couple of hours and then leave. But Melisa said to me, 'What are you doing now? Where are you working?' I was working in a nursing home. And your mom said that they missed me, and Evin wanted me to come back. I said I would consider it. I wasn't sure with Jennifer there, with all of the drama and crap. But they said they were with a new nursing agency and Jennifer wasn't working as much. So, I said I'd think about it. Then I got a call from the new agency and I thought I might as well fill out the paperwork. Within a month, the agency called me to work for you again. And when Jennifer found out I was coming back, she quit." "That was the end of the soap opera."

"Even though we had to deal with many problems together, one of my fondest memories, which I'll never forget was watching you dance in a wheelchair. I was coming in the door to do my shift. As I was coming in, approaching the dining area, you were on the other side of the table and you were dancing to "Sexy Boy" by Sean Michaels. You didn't see me. I just stopped and watched you. You were moving the chair sideways, back and forth, turning around in circles, singing, bouncing your head … OMG. The wheelchair wasn't stopping you from dancing. You know when you see a kid do something for the first time. I could never fathom you dancing; I got tears in my eyes. It was the most beautiful moment ever … you were being yourself. You were free."

Kathy and Shawn

Chapter 21

BREAKING THE RULES

"Higher Dad! I Love to Fly"

S hawn laid a plate of baked sole with a lemon-butter sauce, hush puppies and spinach on my table. "Eeww, is that spinach?" I asked. "Just let me finish," says Shawn, putting some sauce on the vegetable. "Don't make me grimace!" I said. "Don't get me started," says Shawn. "It smells like you farted," replied Evin. "That's cause I sharted," joked Shawn. "You're so 'tarded'", I offered, suddenly moving my chair up and forward so I could get in a glancing head-butt against Shawn's ball cap, which knocks up the visor. "Close," says Shawn, who straightens up and resets his hat, "but no cigar."

Shawn, one of my long-time nurses, never takes his hat off. Shawn claims that if I ever knocked it off, he'll quit. My goal is to see if Shawn will actually quit if I knocked it off. I have been trying for eight years. So far, Shawn is undefeated. At 42, and not at all an imposing presence, Shawn is still lean and strong enough to lift me easily. Possibly balding, somewhat nearsighted (the glasses are always on), his most distinctive physical feature is his left arm. It has a huge vein that snakes its way up his forearm like the wall of China, making it appear at a glance (because you wouldn't want to stare) as if his entire arm were a curvy process slapped out of wet clay. Shawn said he doesn't want to fix it surgically. As a teen, Shawn had kidney failure, dialysis and almost lost an eye. He received a transplant kidney from his mother when he was 25. He says the arm is there to remind him. After the transplant, Shawn was enrolled in vocational rehabilitation. Though his first love is cooking, he decided to go to nursing school to get his RN degree. At first, he worked in pediatrics. Babies! In fact, before me, Shawn had never had a significant relationship with a disabled person.

Shawn said his nursing agency was sending him all over the place and he heard there was a client really close by his home. He kept bugging them to let him try. Finally, they sent him to orientation with me, but they said, 'Just be prepared; this patient is a real pain in the ass. A lot of people don't get along with him.' Shawn came to see me and we just sat and talked, and when we were done he then said, 'When do I start?' We are now close, like brothers. Shawn has stayed with me through three different agencies. We even got our pierced ears together. We were supposed to get tattoos together, when my fraternity got chartered, but Shawn chickened out. "I couldn't," says Shawn. "Cause you're a wimp," I said. "Cause I'm immunosuppressed," says Shawn.

This was Shawn's first nursing agency. Just as there can be problems and conflicts with and between individual nurses, a poorly run nursing agency can also cause misery. To cover a client who needs 24-hour nursing, the agency must provide enough trained nurses to not only cover all of the shifts, but also cover for nurses who don't show up, those who get sick, go on vacation or quit. While we used this particular agency, their nurses would often be late, sometimes not show up, or sometimes just not be able to handle the job. As a result, Mom was constantly afraid to leave for work or would sometimes have to rush back home.

When Shawn needed a substitute the agency sent random nurses who had never been to my house and weren't oriented and didn't know how to take care of me. New nurses were supposed to have eight hours of orientation to learn how to care for a patient with a trach and a vent. They would hire new people instead of paying overtime to one of my regular, experienced nurses.

I knew this was true because of his own efforts to reschedule nurses. Although the agency's rules forbade me to have my nurses' contact information, the nurses gave their numbers to me anyway. When somebody couldn't make it and the agency would tell me that none of his regular substitute nurses were available, I would call the regulars myself. The nurses would say the agency had not called them, and they were available. I would then call the agency and say, "So-and-so is available and will be coming in this afternoon." The agency would get so angry! The whole thing was infuriating and frustrating. My family was looking for a new nursing agency when the agency abruptly dropped me. Fortunately, we'd already found a new and better agency to use.

It was just one of those situations, says my Mom, when you don't realize the stress you're under until it's gone. With the new agency, we didn't have to worry about scheduling and they had more qualified nurses. If the family made a complaint, the agency took care of it right away. "It was like a breath of fresh air," says mom. In the beginning the new agency didn't have nurses trained to take care of ventilator patients, so most of my nurses followed me from the old agency to the new one. Nurses were permitted to drive me wherever I needed to go, and Shawn began taking me to school. Shawn said I loved school, except for the times he fell asleep in class and started to snore. In which case, I would gently smack Shawn with my wheelchair.

Because he lived so close, Shawn was the emergency go-to guy. One time when Kathy was on night shift, she called Shawn at three in the morning. Initially he didn't answer. Shawn said that normally when he goes to sleep it takes a nuclear bomb to rouse him. Kathy was panicking. She had pulled my trach tube out to change it and she couldn't get it back in. Shawn jumped in his car, drove ten minutes, popped my tube back in and went home. Shawn says my trach is not your typical trach because my neck isn't straight.

Ever so often Kathy and Shawn would take me on a long- distance trip to see my family or friends. He drove to Memphis and got to meet all of my old friends from MDA camp, the counselors, and some of my church friends. Shawn said those trips were always a blast because he'd heard a lot of stories and had seen pictures. Now he got to meet those people. And of course, there was also the food: barbecue, catfish, hush puppies. Shawn says food is his Zanex. No matter how bad things get, he can always just go into the kitchen and fix something to eat.

After five great years with this nursing agency, something abruptly changed. It seemed to be under new management. All of a sudden,the agency's nurses were no longer allowed to drive me or any other patient with a trach. For me, it felt like the gates of prison had just slammed in my face. Neither my family nor the nurses could understand it. I was not fragile. I wasn't even trach dependent: I could breathe up to eight hours on my own. The agency's nurses could still drive other clients without trachs. Why was I so different?

I could get a driver for my doctors' appointments but I had to arrange it two weeks in advance. It just wasn't working. I broke a tooth and needed to see the dentist immediately. The dentist was only five minutes away and even though it was an emergency, the agency still insisted that Shawn couldn't drive me. It's not like I could call Uber! I needed an especially equipped van and we owned an especially equipped van. What I needed was a driver. My family offered to indemnify the agency for anything that might happen when a nurse drove but they were unyielding. They suggested that my family hire a driver. But how could they hire a driver to be available once in a while at irregular times? And, of course, there was always that ubiquitous and sexist suggestion that Mom should quit her job-that wasn't an option either.

From there, the rules kept changing willy-nilly, and they got increasingly onerous. The agency insisted that I wear a pulse oximeter, the "Pulsox," which clips onto a finger and measures the oxygen saturation in the blood. I didn't want to, and my doctor told the agency it was not necessary. They responded that their rules superseded the doctor's orders. They even had their doctor call my doctor to persuade him differently. Next, they said the nurses could not remove my ventilator machine at all. They did this regularly so I could breathe on my own and exercise my lungs and muscles. Once again, the agency insisted I had to do something that didn't comply with my doctor's orders.

The agency insisted on a video camera in my bedroom or that a nurse be in the bedroom with me all night instead of in the next room with a baby monitor. Another new rule stipulated that a nurse could not follow me on a bicycle when I went for a ride around the neighborhood in my wheelchair. However, I had to stay within sight of my nurse at all times. This meant, of course, that I couldn't ride around my neighborhood in my wheelchair unless my nurse happened to be a 'marathon' runner. It was like they were trying to control my whole life! It went from 'Let us provide nurses so you can have the life you want' to 'Let us provide nurses so you can have the life we want you to have.' They were taking away my rights as a person.

It went on this way for months. My family was really getting fed up with this agency and the agency was getting fed up with us. Then one day it all careened to a screeching halt. Shawn and my mom were meeting with the agency in Clearwater on a Monday. We were trying to convince them that I didn't need all these extra rules. We told them that I would go to a pulmonologist to get all of the orders clarified. They knew that I was doing this doctor's appointment on their behalf.

Initially the appointment was months away. We kept calling and finally got an appointment only a few days away. We called the agency to let them know on which day and time the appointment was scheduled, yet when the time came there was no driver. Shawn called the agency and was told we had not requested a driver and it would take at least an hour for someone to show up. We couldn't wait – we would lose the appointment. Shawn told the agency that we would get my brother Nathan to drive. Unfortunately, Nathan was near comatose with sleep and refused to get up. Then Shawn made a mistake. He decided to drive me himself. The appointment had already been rescheduled once and after all. All of this was for the agency anyway. The agency had known about the appointment but hadn't sent a driver! What could be the harm? Shawn had been driving me for years.

The agency called Shawn again and he pretended Nathan was with us. Shawn later said that it was a bad decision but he was in race-mode. He admitted later he should have just called the doctor's office and told them we'd be late.

Shawn and I arrived safely and went into the doctor's office for the appointment. The doctor was laughing at all of the agency's rules. The doctor wrote out a full page of orders and specified that since I was able to breath off the vent for eight hours a day, I didn't need a Pulsox or any of the other measures that the agency was insisting upon. As we left the doctor's office and got back into the van, Shawn and I saw a large man lumbering toward them. It was Patrick,the agency's clinical director. He called out for Shawn to stop. We were busted! Patrick got on the phone with the agency, then told Shawn that he, Patrick, was going to drive us home. And that Shawn was fired, effective immediately! Another nurse was coming in to cover Shawn's shift. Shawn didn't say another word the whole way back to my house. He was in shock. I told him not to worry and that mom and I would take care of it. I was arguing with Patrick. I asked him, "Why didn't the agency have a driver for me? They knew I had this appointment. They knew I needed a driver. This appointment had been for the agency's benefit anyway.' Patrick said, "Oh, right, all this was my fault." When we got back to the house Shawn sat down with Patrick and me at the table. Patrick asked Shawn if he had anything to say. Shawn replied, "What is there to say? We had a scheduled doctor's appointment you knew about and yet a driver wasn't scheduled. I took Evin, you caught me, and now you're firing me. It just doesn't benefit anyone. Patrick gave Shawn the agency's exit interview papers. He had them with him all along. Shawn couldn't handle it and he just walked outside.

At the time my mom wasn't home. A little later Erin, the agency's area director, and Leslie, the local director, arrived at my house. But by that time, I was nowhere to be found. I had taken off! I was so furious. I kept riding until I was out of our neighborhood's community. Shawn said Leslie and Erin started panicking, telling him to call 911. Shawn got on a bike and found me. We talked, and he convinced me to come back to the house. Inside, we all talked about the doctor's new set of orders, but again, Leslie, Erin and Patrick insisted that their rules superseded the doctor's orders. Patrick was an R.N. so we felt he had no right to say the doctor's orders didn't make sense.

Then a car pulled up outside. It was Jo. She was there to take Shawn's place. She's actually a very sweet nurse but I wasn't having it. I headed for the door and the agency people started shouting... "Where are you going?" "Are you now making a law that I can't go into my own back yard?", I shouted! Everybody ran outside into the driveway. I wanted to hit somebody or something. I was staring at Erin. They were saying that they cared about me but I knew they didn't or they wouldn't be doing this. I started driving full speed in my wheelchair right at them. Then, at the last minute, I turned and ran into my own van. They were asking, "Are you OK?" I'm like, "Yeah, I'm OK. You just turned my whole world upside down. What you are doing is causing me to want to end my life!" As I started riding off again, Erin shouted to me that I'd better not leave the premises! I replied, I'll do whatever the hell I want. And I drove on into the street in front of the house. She then yelled that she would have to call 911, and that I'd have to go to the hospital.

Shawn (who claims that he and I are just alike and neither of us can keep his mouth shut) started arguing with them. He bitterly told them that they didn't care about him or me and they certainly didn't want what's best for me. He told them this was all about liability. Erin looked Shawn dead in the eye and told him they we're doing this because they cared about me, loved me and we're doing this for my safety. Down the street, my battery started to fail. The argument sputtered to a stalemate. Shawn came to fix the battery and bring me home. Patrick, Erin and Leslie went back to the agency. Jo, the nurse I didn't want, stayed with Shawn and me until Mom got home.

Mom started making phone calls, trying to get Shawn reinstated. Shawn had never, in his entire career, had one complaint or infraction. Shawn kept going to my house, helping and hiding out. He didn't want to tell his wife he'd been fired, and he felt sure he'd be reinstated. He was right. When Mom finally contacted the founder-owner of the agency and had told him the whole story, he gave Shawn his job back.

But after that, they were "gunning" for Shawn. The local agency team resented the appeal and the interference of the agency's owner. It was just after 7 a.m., a few days after Shawn had been reinstated, that my Pulsox kept going off. It was because I wasn't wearing it and Shawn had turned it off. His lunch was in his hands when the door bell rang.

It was the scheduling guy from the agency. He did not have permission to just come straight into the house but he walked in as Shawn was putting his lunch away. Shawn asked him, "What's up?" He said this was a random spot check to make sure every thing's OK. He noticed that Shawn didn't have his shoes on. He later got a call saying he'd be fired if he didn't keep his shoes on in the house.

A few days later, there was knock at the door. Anthony, one of my regular nurses, answered it. Mom saw Anthony walk in with Leslie from the agency following him. Mom was outraged. She was really angry. She got into Leslie's face and said, 'Maybe you can control the nurses in my house but you can't come in here without my permission.' Anthony was scared. He was scared of mom fighting with the agency and worried about his own job. He didn't have on his shoes.

Mom was livid about the new "spot checks." On top of all the usual stress, now she had the agency continuously and at any moment invading the privacy of her home. She started looking for another agency. Not long after that, the agency called Shawn while I was at school. They said he was getting too close to me. The nurse shouldn't get too close to the client, they said. They told Shawn they might have to pull him off my case. He felt they were angry and were watching him through a microscope.

It took only a few months more before there was another incident with a driver. This time it was over mutual complaints and accusations. As a result, Shawn was fired for good. "I'm the crier, not you," Shawn says to me, grinning. "Like that day I got fired from the agency. I came in and told you I loved you and that we'd always be friends. Saying goodbye was creepy, like somebody died. I felt helpless, hopeless and so betrayed even though I was doing the right thing. It all crumbled so quickly."

By then, my family had found another agency. It was called Consumer Direct. Consumer Direct is an agency that allows clients to manage the hiring, firing, training, and scheduling of their own professionals. I felt like we finally found a solution that works for us. An agency that enables me to take control of my own life and nursing services. Although Consumer Direct paid more, to their employees, they did not provide health insurance. That terrified Shawn; his wife was ill and could no longer work, and he himself needed ongoing medical care. But it turned out that he was able, with several of my other nurses, to successfully transfer to the new agency. Shawn now gets medical insurance through the Visiting Nurses Association.

Anthony thinks the whole agency fiasco could have been avoided if we had just obeyed the rules. He said he didn't think it was wrong for an agency to change their rules and that we shouldn't have broken those rules. He said we should do what the rules say until we can change them. I then told him; Rosa Parks broke a rule. She sat in the front of the bus. Anthony said thank God we don't need to break rules like that any more. Yes, Anthony, I said. We still do.

Shawn & Anthony

Chapter 22

MILESTONES...KICKING AND SCREAMING

Proud Mom

When I was younger, I achieved milestones because I was pushed into unfamiliar and uncomfortable situations. It wasn't until later that I achieved goals because I understood that I really could achieve something. It took some growing up before I understood how important it was to push myself.

For example, I never really wanted to go to college. I was just doing it because my parents said I had to go. As a young person, I never heard of anyone with a disability like mine who went to college other than Stephen Hawking. And Hawking was an able-bodied person while he went to college which gave him a big head-start. It made me think I had to be freakishly intelligent to be successful. I wasn't the only one who felt that way. I had many disabled friends and they found college intimidating, too. How do you take notes, go to the bathroom, get a drink of water, or eat lunch? How will you deal with the stares and whispers of "normal" people?

Kappa Sigma Fraternity

Even Harry, my best friend from MD camp, who was outgoing, optimistic and had a strong passion for learning new things was afraid of college. He wanted to go but he was too scared. It wasn't like he wasn't smart enough - A's and Harry were meant to be together. He had a 4.0 in school for as long as I could remember. When Harry spoke, you could tell he knew what he was talking about. If he didn't, he would by the end of the day.

But going to college helped me see how immature I actually was compared to my peers. For example, I didn't know how to be organized. I understood that everybody starts out very disorganized, but I didn't even know that I needed folders to carry papers. I certainly didn't know which folder was needed for which class. I didn't know about buying textbooks or where I'd go to buy a textbook.

It was frustrating to be a college man and yet still needing to ask for help with trivial things like getting a drink of water. Who was I? What was I? I didn't know how to speak to people my own age. I was used to speaking to children or elderly people. When it came to people my own age, I didn't understand what they were doing. I didn't know what to say after, "Hello, my name is Evin." My mind went blank.

I came from an entirely different world that my peers had never seen or experienced. I felt embarrassed to leave class to use the restroom. I wasn't used to making my own decisions. Everything felt wrong – as if I was going to be punished for breaking rules that didn't exist anymore. Can you imagine how disappointed I was in myself? I doubted I would ever catch up. I was just showing up for classes and going home - living this way made me feel ever more hopeless. Not only was there little intellectual stimulation at community college, I didn't feel like I had any kind of independence that you expect when you go to college.

Plus it seemed that my father had taken micromanaging my affairs to the next level. I felt he expected me to do everything he said 100 percent. Primarily to keep the peace, I tried to accept that this was just the way he was - but having to live at home while I was in college was the last straw. Little by little, I tried to assert myself as an adult. My nurses were helping me to grow and branch away from my parents and make my own decisions. However, my dad sometimes didn't like the decisions I made. One of my first stands that I made for myself had to do with church. I was tired of going every Sunday but my father was telling me I had to go with the family. I was told to go to church every Sunday and I was told where to go. I knew my father cared about me and my soul. But I also knew that now that I was an adult, it was my responsibility, not his.

One Sunday morning, Kathy was working to fill in on the day shift. My dad asked Kathy why I wasn't awake. Kathy told my dad that I had said I was sick and didn't want to get up. My dad came into my room to ask me why I wasn't up and I told him I didn't feel well. My dad believed me and went to church with my mother without me. But really, I just didn't want to go. When my dad got home from church, he asked how I felt since I was playing video games and I told him that I was better. He didn't look pleased but said nothing more.

After that, my dad stopped telling me to go to church but he still tried to 'guilt trip' me into going. He would come to my room every Saturday night and ask me several random questions that he didn't really seem interested in- about my video games, or movies, or other things. But the last question of the evening would always be the same: "Will your mother and I see you at church tomorrow?" It seemed as if that was the question he was really interested in my answering, not the others. There was an undertone, a meaning, like he was trying to make sure I would go. It was the way he'd look at me to see if I was going to come or not. Finally, I got fed up. I said, "Dad, stop. First off, I don't come to church for you and mom. I go to church for God. So don't keep asking me whether I'm going or not. You are pressuring and guilting me." After that, Dad understood and backed off.

Another important milestone came after an argument between my dad and me. I was trying to explain to Dad that I had to be free to make my own decisions and my own mistakes. We were going back and forth, getting very heated. Both of our voices were raised. Suddenly, I felt like there was no getting through to him. I got very upset and overwhelmed with how little control I had over my own life.

Bachelor Degree Graduation

When I went back to my room sobbing, Kathy tried to console me but there was no consolation and I told her I was thinking about suicide. What was the point of living a life if I couldn't be an independent human being? I had no meaning or purpose of my own. The next day Kathy talked to my parents and then I talked to my mom. I told her about how it's my life and if I want to eat badly, sin, procrastinate, waste my life away, that it was my choice and not my dad's.

Now I can understand a little better about how hard it must be for the parent of a disabled child to let go. My mother understood. She talked to my father and he began to loosen up.

My mother, who was very stressed by all the turmoil in the house, took me to a doctor who diagnosed me with major depression and prescribed antidepressant medication. Naturally, in keeping with how difficult I was, I refused to take it. I said I didn't want it and I didn't need it. I hated medications. I never would take medication whether it was getting a flu shot or Tylenol or anything. Whatever would come my way, I wanted to deal with it using my natural immune system. Sometimes when you take too much medication, your body becomes dependent on the medication and loses its natural immunity. But I had no idea how much depression was affecting every aspect of my life and the people around me. Depression prevented me from moving forward.

At this point I had 24 hour nursing but I was running nurses off left and right. I would be difficult – impatient, angry and rude. I was bitter. When friends or family came to visit, I'd have to be the center of attention. I'd cause drama and make rude comments and then say, "I'm just being honest." I thought I could say whatever I wanted to whomever I wanted.

Each new nurse who came needed training and if a new nurse wasn't trained, my mom would be afraid to leave the house to go to work. The nurses who stayed like Lois, Jennifer and Kathy were always fighting. (Shawn was working nights and steered clear of the drama.) It was hell on my mother.

Sometimes with depression you have to have someone who cares about you to help motivate you. You are in such negative, angry denial that you don't have the ability to motivate yourself or make good decisions. I was definitely in that state. When you're in that state, the only way to get out of it is with help. Help came in the way of an ultimatum. One day my mother called me into her home office. She was at her wit's end. She told me I needed to take the antidepressant medication and I refused. Then she shouted at me, "Take your medication or GET THE F__ _ OUT OF MY HOUSE!" That was pretty shocking. She said she couldn't stand the drama and the stress in the house any more. It was her home yet she found no refuge in it. I was dragging everyone down this hole of depression. Between my nurses' conflicts, my anger and depression, my mom was reaching her breaking point. She could not take my attitude and negativity any longer. When she calmed down a little, she said, "I'm your mother and I love you. Do you trust me?" And I said, "Yes." She said, "Do you believe I have your best interest at heart?" I said, " I did." So Mom made a deal with me. She said to try the medication for 30 days and if it didn't work, we'd throw it away and find another avenue or another solution to this problem. But she also said, "Take it for 30 days or just get out."

I knew she meant it. I was lucky to have a mother who was strong enough and loved me enough to give me an ultimatum. The medication was a huge help. I took it for 30 days and never threw it away. I still take anti-depressant medication today. For me, it was one of the puzzle pieces that have helped me put together a meaningful life.

Chapter 23

LOSING HARRY

Harry

I was just finishing my third semester at Pasco Hernando Community College. It was Dec 2, 2008, a quiet day between Thanksgiving and Christmas. I was playing a video game in my "man cave" when my mother came in and told me that Harry had passed away.

I couldn't believe it. Harry and I had spent our last summer together in MD camp over a year ago just before my family moved to Florida. He had seemed fine. I was in shock. I was terrified. We were both just 19 years old. One week earlier, I'd had an extremely vivid and detailed dream that Harry had died. It was so real that when I awoke, I thought maybe it had really happened. So I wondered - would it have made a difference if I'd told someone about my dream? I know it wouldn't have but Harry's death in far away Arkansas seemed surreal.

Harry's death was shocking not just to me but to everyone. Harry, who had Duchenne's MD, had seemed pretty healthy most of his life. Unlike some, he'd hardly ever been in a hospital. Until a few months ago, Harry hadn't experienced any of the common health problems with his heart or lungs that are commonly associated with Duchenne's. Some kids have that kind of trouble by the age of 11 or 12. Harry's breathing was affected by the disease but never bad enough to go to the hospital.

In early June of that year, Harry "coded" for the first time: He went into respiratory distress. In other words, he just stopped breathing and passed out. EMS came, intubated him, and took him to the hospital. Once in the hospital, he recovered and could breathe on his own again. The doctors put him on medication and sent him home. Then approximately a week later, he coded again and was back in the hospital.

When you suffer respiratory distress, if somebody doesn't get you breathing again pretty quickly, your heart stops. After that, brain damage can begin - the more frequent and/or longer the episodes, the greater the chance of brain damage. So although he didn't need a tracheotomy and a ventilator machine to breath, the doctors wanted to give Harry a trache anyway. They felt he would have more and more episodes and it could end badly. Harry's mom and dad wanted him to do it. But Harry was terrified. He didn't want a trache. For most of us with MD, it seems like the beginning of the end.

Harry and I were similar in many ways. However, there was one big difference. I liked to try new things. Harry was afraid to step outside his comfort zone. He liked to sleep - I hated to sleep. Harry would be back at the cabin while I would be dancing with the girls. Harry wanted to try new things but he was afraid. He was thoughtful. I was impulsive. I'd say why not go for it; Harry would say no. I think the difference was that I tried to make the world adapt to me; Harry tried to withdraw instead. Subconsciously, I didn't want my disability to define me. Harry didn't want to make waves.

Harry's parents wanted Harry to get the trache because they knew without it, he may soon die. But unlike me, Harry hadn't been all that sick. He hadn't had the near-death experiences I'd had. He hadn't suffered from carbon dioxide poisoning like I had. I'd been disabled from birth and it was all I knew. Harry started out as a relatively healthy boy who slowly became more and more disabled. He just wasn't ready to acknowledge that the trache was really necessary, even though his parents knew that it was.

Miss Betty, our "mom" from MDA camp, sat with Harry the Saturday and Sunday before the trache operation. Harry was very upset. They called me to talk with him about the trache operation. I gave Harry a pep talk. I told him that although I hated my trache at first, I had to admit that it had actually made my life much better. I had tons more energy after having the operation and I was much healthier as well. Harry seemed to feel a lot better after we talked. But later on, he got very scared, very upset again. One thing I know is that physically a trache is hard on anyone. But if you don't acknowledge it as necessary and accept the pain and the problems associated with it, it will be so much worse. Survival with MD is a mind-game. As Miss Betty says, your mind-set is 99.9 percent of survival.

After the operation, Harry never talked again. He never adjusted to it. He'd panic at the drop of a hat. He just stayed in bed all the time. Miss Betty and another MD camp counselor visited Harry a month after the operation. Miss Betty said he couldn't calm down. His anxiety level was so high, she was afraid the stress might bring on a heart attack. Privately she broke down crying. She told the other counselor she thought Harry may not have more than six months left. But it wasn't his heart that gave out. It was a complication with the trach and vent apparatus, a complication that could happen to anyone, including me. The story made me speechless and scared.

Harry was at home with his stepdad and his younger brother, Dustin, who also had Duchenne's. His mom, a nurse, was with her mother and sister in Memphis that day. Suddenly, Harry began to hemorrhage blood. There was blood everywhere. So much so fast that it was hard to tell its origin. It was bursting from Harry's trach. Harry's stepfather, Vance, got Harry into the bedroom and started to suction out the blood. They called 911. They called Miss Betty and Harry's mom to come home right away. They didn't realize it but Harry was already gone. The trache had been pressing and rubbing on the wall of a vein in Harry's throat. The constant pressure caused a portion of the vein wall to weaken. It finally burst. Technically, it is called a tracheo-arterial fistula. It is rare but it can happen. It usually results in death.

Harry's passing affected his family deeply. His younger brothers, Dustin, and Vance, were right beside him as he choked on his own blood. Not being able to do anything, they watched him die. Harry's mother felt guilty about not being there at the time. I once overheard her saying she felt that maybe she could have done something. But in truth, there was nothing she or anyone could have done.

Harry's mother became silent and was unable to speak for at least a year and a half. I remember driving up to Marion, Arkansas for the funeral a few days after his passing. I remember rushing to get everything ready because there was no question about it - I was going to be there. The whole drive up, I felt like I was in a bad dream. Any moment I would wake and things would be back to the way they had been. I remember pulling up to the funeral home door with my mother to support me. My father would have been there too, but unfortunately, he was still in Afghanistan. They opened the doors and I drove forward in my chair. My heart felt like it had stopped: This was exactly the dream I'd had two weeks earlier. Every detail was the same, from the people behind me to where Harry's casket was situated. Throughout the funeral, I kept thinking this just isn't real. I was more shocked than I was upset by the whole situation.

It's always in the back of my mind that today might be my last day. For people who are disabled like Harry and me, there is always a higher risk that we might die young. Harry and I always tried to be optimistic. But due to our fear, there were so many things we chose not to do. Things we could have taken advantage of or capitalized on to further our lives ... for ourselves and for those around us. So toward the end of the funeral, instead of going into denial and depression, I had an epiphany.

I did not want this to happen to me. I'm not talking about dying young because that's always a possibility. Harry had all of the tools to be successful but he allowed his disability and the obstacles to overwhelm him. He always said he wanted to go to college but in the end he was too scared. Like Harry, fear was causing me to be more disabled than I actually was. When I was a teenager, sometimes the thought of college would make me feel panicky – it would cause my heart to race. Harry could have easily gone to college. He was way more intelligent than me. He had a higher IQ and he was even more physically able than me. But he was afraid. I suddenly realized that I didn't want to go to college because I was afraid that I would not succeed.

My epiphany was that I wasn't giving my all in everything I did. If Harry had given his all, he would have been more successful than I have ever been. I didn't want to live life not giving 120 percent. If I gave 120 percent and failed, I'd be happy. But I'll never know if I don't at least start. I had to focus on working toward a goal, regardless of my fear.

Harry and Friends

Harry's death changed me. I had no real ambition before Harry's death. But when I experienced how all that potential in Harry was just gone, it gave me a kind of motivation I'd never felt before. The memory of my own respiratory failure and my near-death experience came back to me like a hammer blow. I remembered all the images and feelings - that indescribable light. I remembered the peace, the certainty of God and the afterlife, the way God is always with me. I realized it wasn't about what I wanted to do. It wasn't even about what I wanted. It was deeper than that. I felt like if an opportunity came my way, whether I wanted to do this thing or not, I should go for it. I decided that whatever came my way, if I could do it, I would do it.

I know Harry felt he just didn't have the resources to be successful. But I've come to see that you have to do what you can do. If I can only do 10 percent, hell, I'm going to go out and do that 10 percent as well as I can. **This became my motto: If I can do it, I will.** I went back to community college with a new attitude and earned my Associate's Degree.

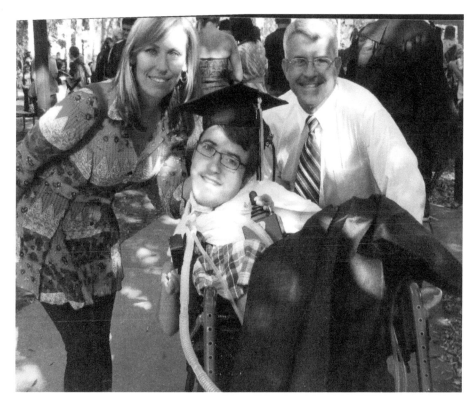

Associates Degree

Chapter 24

LOOKING FOR MY FUTURE

Comicon

I became ambitious. I became obnoxious. I wish I could say I became saint-like after the experience of Harry's death and the reaffirmation of my own near-death experience, but that's not what happened. It was all another stepping stone toward being grateful for what I've got.

It was while I was at community college that my nurse Shawn first came on board. He could see how I was struggling with my relationship with my dad. He told me about healing his relationship with his own father and encouraged me to try to be appreciative of what I had. Shawn's dad had left their home when he was young and Shawn had a hard time getting over the resentment. Finally, he says, he realized that his father was always going to be his father and he didn't really know the circumstances of his father's absence. But he wanted to have a relationship with his father, so he had to let go of the resentments.

Over time, Shawn helped me see that while my dad was a strict disciplinarian and a Marine through and through, he really loved his family and wanted the best. A big turning point came when one day I asked my dad to go out to lunch with me. We went out to a sushi place and had a good time together. What surprised me was how much it meant to my dad. While we were out, he said, "You know, this is pretty special. This is the first time you've ever asked me to do something with you." Today, my father and I have a strong and loving relationship. I am no longer afraid of him. It was only recently that I let my dad know how afraid I was of him when I was younger. He was really surprised and I could tell it truly bothered him to find out. He apologized with tears in his eyes and said he had always simply tried to be the best dad he knew how to be. He wanted to teach and train his three sons how to be better prepared for life, both now and eternally. We were both are glad we'd opened up and shared these feelings.

Another part of the puzzle was – what was I going to do with my life? I couldn't imagine a career for myself. What could I do? How could I become independent? My parents told me early on if I couldn't find anything to do or if I couldn't get through college, I could live with them. Now, I love my parents, but there was no way I was going to be one of those people who lives with his parents his entire life. I wanted to go out into the world and experience it on my own. I still do and I'm still working toward that goal. As I neared the completion of my Associate's Degree, I felt more and more discouraged. I felt I wasn't good at anything. I was having a hard time finding a niche in which someone with my disability could excel.

Because of my lack of physical ability, everything I considered seemed impossible. I looked at being a lawyer and doing legal things because I am good at arguing and I care about justice. But due to all of the physical paperwork you have to do at the beginning of law, before you're able to get an assistant, it seemed impossible. I thought maybe I could be a professor or a teacher, but again, having to handle lots of paperwork, reading and responding to student papers seemed extremely difficult for someone in my position. Virtually any entry-level job like working in a fast food restaurant wasn't in the cards for me, either.

I turned it over and over in my mind and absolutely nothing seemed possible. for me. "Enjoy him while you have him," Shawn said. That really got to me. I tried to understand Dad and really pay attention to the things he did that frustrated me. I had to learn to just let it go. Plus, once my older brother Alex and his wife Lindsey had kids, my dad really changed. He relaxed a lot more. He wasn't in charge of discipline and he could enjoy the fun stuff with his grandkids. It seemed to me he got more approachable - less intimidating. Or maybe, I was just growing up - maturing.

Finally, I felt I was at the end of my search. I was done! I had never truly given up before in my life. But this time was different. I was quitting. I was tired of searching and coming up with disappointing results. What had happened to my plan to change things? Was I letting Harry down by just giving up? It seemed easier to give up after all.

I was completely at the end when I turned to the One many turn to when they're ready to quit. I went to bed that night and prayed: "God, I know you want me to do something with my life. I don't want to go back on my promise to Harry that I'd try to excel in life, when he was unable to reach his goals. I'm done looking. Tomorrow, if I can't find something, then I'm done with college. I'm overwhelmed and can't take it anymore. Please just show me something I can do in this world and I won't question it. I will accept it and do it. I need your help. Amen."

I woke the next morning to go to a therapy appointment with my psychologist. I'd been seeing this psychologist for the past year and half due to my depression. Something about this appointment was different. I realized I was answering my own questions, assessing and fixing my own problems. As I left the appointment, I asked myself: Why can't I do this? I hadn't been using the one organ that God had given me that actually works well – my brain.

Psychology had been a part of my life for a very long time. In that moment, I realized psychology was something I could do. Throughout my whole life, people have reacted differently to me than to others. People of all races, genders, ages, religions and levels of ability seemed to bring their problems to me. So many people feel comfortable talking to me about anything and everything.

I think that in the opinion of many I'm a blank slate. I'm not white; I'm not young; I'm not male … I'm disabled. Girls sometimes talk to me about the most intimate, private things within minutes of meeting me, sometimes about things they haven't even told their friends.

It's like my sex isn't male; it's "disabled." Alpha males can be vulnerable with me. My wheelchair gives people the sense that I am not threatening. I had been talking to people about their problems and trying to give advice for years. Why not do it professionally?

I realized psychology was a good choice for me because of my life experience as well. Despite my youth, I'd experienced more than many who are much older. Living with a disability, you go through many different traumatic and awkward events that others may never experience. I've had to overcome discrimination, abandonment, humiliation, questions about my sexuality in conflict with my religion, depression, loss, death of friends and my own near-death experiences.

My nurses, my parents and I started to search for which universities had good psychology programs somewhat close to my home. We found St. Leo University near Dade City, Florida. It was within driving distance of my house. It was easy for me to get into the school academically and my credits from community college could be transferred without a problem.

I was all set to go on to the next stage in life. Little did I know how much more growing up I still had to do.

Celebrating Birthday Super Hero Style

Chapter 25

REALITY CHECK

Hanging with Nathan and Dad

My first semester at St. Leo's was a disaster. Yes, I was now ambitious and determined to succeed. I believed I had a purpose in life. But my attitude was terrible, my behavior was horrible, and I almost flunked out.

I remember the first day, bumbling around trying to find the disability office. It took a long time; the disability office was on the second floor of a building that was only moderately handicapped accessible. It had electronic doors but the elevator was about the size of a shower. I couldn't turn my wheelchair around. I met with "Miss Chris", the Disabilities Office Coordinator and she gave me paperwork to give to my teachers about accommodations that I needed.

I learned very quickly that a university is different from a community college. Things are much more fast-paced, more demanding, by the book and set in stone. I had to be more focused; I couldn't just slide through. The teachers really wanted to teach their students. They were passionate about their subjects and the students couldn't slack off.

At first, I didn't understand how things worked. It was all very intense. Everyone had a goal-somewhere to go. I was a daytime student now instead of being in school at night. There was so much more to do on campus: activities and as well as classes. I'd floated through community college. But at St. Leo's, my classes were much more demanding. As I sat in class, even as the professors were introducing the material, I felt I wasn't ready. It felt like I was a child being thrown into a room with a bunch of adults. I was much further behind than I had ever anticipated.

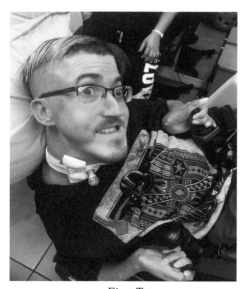

First Tattoo

In one of my first classes, a psychology course, the professor used the chalkboard for everything. Dr. B. was a bit old fashioned and didn't use the Internet which would have made it much easier for me. He began by writing a lot of information on the board. I was following along fairly well until Dr. B. said to the class, "Before I erase this, does anyone else need to write it down?" I couldn't write anything down, so I said, "Sir, I'm not done with the notes yet." Dr. B. said, "OK, let me know when you're done and I'll erase it."

I was expecting him to notice my disability. I'm thinking: Can't he see that I can't write? I couldn't even lift my arm to raise my hand. A few minutes later, I mustered the courage to again raise my voice and say, "Sir, I can't write anything at all." Dr. B. said, "And how is that my problem?" I was shocked. I'd never heard a response like that in my life. Usually people are just so helpful and accommodating. It took me aback. But it made me angry, too. I said, "Sir, it's your problem because I'm supposed to take the test. How can I take the test if I can't take the notes?" He kind of looked at me and went, "I don't know. What do you want me to do?" I said, "You have notes right there in your hand. You could photocopy those." Dr. B. said, "No, I don't do that." I said, "You could assign a student to take notes or copy your notes." I was getting more and more angry and even more incredulous. Dr. B. said again, this wasn't his problem. I said, "It is your problem because my parents are paying for me to come to this school and get an education. I can't get an education if I can't study for the test. If I can't study for the test, I will fail the test. If I fail the test, I will fail your class. If I fail your class, it could reflect badly on you." Dr. B. began to argue with me and I said, "Listen, Mr. B...."He said, "It's Doctor B., not Mister B." And I said, "I'll start calling you Doctor when you start acting like one." Which, I realized, might have been a little disrespectful. The other students in the classroom were staring at us with disbelief. Finally, one of the girls got up and said, "I'll do your notes." She seemed embarrassed for me and whispered in my ear, "I'm sorry." I thanked her and told her I appreciated her offer but asked her to open the door for me instead. "I can't stay in the room with this man anymore," I said.

I headed for the disabilities office and talked to Miss Chris. I was so angry and self-righteous. Miss Chris helped to talk me down and we figured out how I could get the notes from the class. Still, I couldn't believe a professor thought he wasn't there to help me! I wanted to be treated as "normal," but I wanted to be treated as special, too. It was a new concept-being disabled did not make me the center of the universe. This was the first of many conversations in which Miss Chris helped me to mature and improve my attitude. She saved me from many failures. Though I still believe Dr. B. was unnecessarily harsh, it was probably the first time anybody ever expected me to deal with my disability all by myself without his or her help. It was a rude awakening.

That semester was truly a reality check. It was a mental, emotional and physical blow to my ego. I struggled for three months and ended up getting three F's and a D. I didn't even realize I was doing so badly. I thought I was at least a C student. There was a place on line to look up how you were doing but I didn't know about it. My GPA dropped to about a 1.8. The school said you have to bring this up or you will be expelled.

When I think back on why I got those three F's, I believe I just wasn't working hard enough. I was motivated but I didn't know how to succeed in a big university environment as opposed to a community college. I was pushing people away who might have helped me and unaware of just how poor my skills were. I was socially behind and was having lots of uncomfortable and secret feelings about being gay.

I had been able to get people to feel sorry for me my whole life. You would think, while I was at community college, people would be able to tell the difference between taking advantage and really needing help. But it wasn't that easy to tell. Even for me! I would get people to feel so sorry for me and they would help me with anything. Sometimes I needed help but sometimes I was just taking advantage.

When I transferred to St. Leo University, I thought I could do the same thing. I didn't study for tests. I didn't do my homework. I thought people would just feel sorry for me and help me do my work. Reality set in rather quickly because

My Design

a private university works a little differently than a community college. People at this college clearly saw through my B.S..

St. Leo's was willing to help me the way a university helps all its students. They could give me accommodations - a structure that would level the playing field. But instead of accepting their way, I kept trying to do it my way. I guess we all do things that we wish we hadn't done in the past. For me, this was one of those moments. Nobody was going to do the work for me. I had to do it myself. It helped me to grow up and realize that I had to buckle down. I had to stop acting stupid and save playtime for later.

Miss Chris helped me, too. She didn't baby me. She didn't take my B.S.. any more than Dr. B had. She helped me with encouragement and constructive criticism. She laid it out for me - this is what you have to do. She was a lot like a therapist. I would get upset and I'd go to her. She would calm me down and convince me that I could do what I thought I couldn't. I could pass that test! I could write that paper! She was instrumental in getting me through that year.

During the winter break, I prepared myself for the next semester. I changed my mind-set. I decided that I'd study differently and get more organized. The next semester, the school sent me to an extra class once a week that teaches you how to study. I did something right because by the next year, I had straight A's!

Chapter 26

MENTOR, CRITIC, FRIEND

"Miss Chris" speaks of her experiences with Evin…

Miss Chris

I was feeling new," says Christine G., Ph.D., (or "Miss Chris" as Evin fondly calls her). "The year Evin began at St. Leo University, I had just left teaching middle school special education to become St. Leo's new Assistant Director of Disability Services. I later became the Director of Accessibility Services".

"Evin came into my office and proceeded to let me know that he needed accommodations. We went over what it was that he needed. At that time, Evin had a bit of a chip on his shoulder. That's not so surprising. It happens to the handicapped. Look at what they've been through: being separated from their peers into Special Education; suffering the cruelty of other children; abiding frustration and disappointment. When they get here, they don't always want to hear about accommodations. They're angry. They don't want to be different. Why should they?"

"I think Evin had some anger issues back then. That's an opinion, not a diagnosis. I believe he'd never been to a school where they had treated him as if he were just another student. I also don't think he quite knew how to relate. Within days, I received a few emails from Evin's instructors saying that they were having problems. Evin was being argumentative, disrespectful, and answering questions in unhelpful ways."

"Then, one particular professor came in to see me. Professor B. had been in an argument with Evin in class about notes on the blackboard. I just looked at him and said, 'If you're going to be writing on the board, then you have to be able to supply those notes to the student.' It was just common sense. 'Evin has mobility issues and therefore we need to do this.' And the professor said, 'Well, I don't think I should have to do it.' And I said, 'I'm sorry, sir, but you do. A little later, Evin came to my office. He was just furious about his encounter with Professor B. I said, 'I've already taken care of this; don't even worry about it.' And Evin looked at me and said, 'How can you take care of it? He just shows me no respect.' And I said, 'But I don't think you show him any, either.' That's how we met. The professor needed to come to grips but Evin needed to back off, as well. This was the first of many heart-to-heart talks between Evin and me during which we worked on knocking "the chip" off of his shoulder. When Evin came into my office, he knew he was going to be treated as well as he treated me. If he was going to be nasty to me, I was going to turn around and tell him that he could come back when he thought he could be more respectful. I think we hit it off that way because I wouldn't let him get away with it. He was a good guy. I liked him anyway."

"Evin was pugnacious and stubborn. He needed to learn how to pick his battles and with whom. I'll give you a perfect example. We were in a different building at the time. I came out of that building to go to a meeting and Evin was a few students behind me. He was saying some very nasty things as he tried to get around them. He snarled 'Can't you see I'm handicapped and 'Get out of my way!' He was also going lickity-split in his wheelchair. He could go very fast in that wheelchair!"

" I came up behind him and said, 'What do you think you're doing?'" 'I have to get to class,' he said. "'So do they,' I said. 'If you want to get to class, you'll be polite and you'll ask them nicely." 'Excuse me, but I have to get there in a hurry,' he said. "He starts to go, and I say, 'Since when are you handicapped?' And I walked away from him." "Evin came by later and said, 'What do you mean, since when am I handicapped? I'm in a wheelchair! And I said, 'Look, that wheelchair does not make you handicapped. You have a brain in your head. You're here to learn. You're here to do what every other student is here to do. You are not making friends and you are not being respectful to anybody. And yet you demand to be respected. It's a two-way street."

"After that, he started coming in a little more often. We were talking a bit more. Slowly, I saw Evin begin to fit into St. Leo's a little bit better. It took him about a semester. He started to fit in with others. He didn't feel so much like an outsider." "I think he had a rude awakening when he came here. People weren't going to do things for him. But he handled it. He did what he needed to do."

"At that time, St. Leo had other students with disabilities but many were on line. There were only a few studying on campus like Evin. They had never had a student on campus with 'multiple disabilities.' That is, someone in a wheelchair with a trach who couldn't move any part of his body – even to take notes – without help. The tutoring staff had never dealt with anyone with a disability prior to Evin. The tutoring staff and I had to have a little meeting, so to speak. I was advocating for Evin. The rules were that the tutors weren't supposed to be writing out the papers. Some of the professors were concerned that it would be tutors' words and not those of the students. Evin believed that the academic scandal at the University of North Carolina, in which athletes were given unearned credits, made the situation even worse. The tutors just refused to write for him."

"According to Evin, this was a very difficult period for him. He became very angry at the rules which he felt were imbecilic when it came to somebody like him. All of the school's alternate suggestions were totally impracticable for someone like Evin. Speech-to-computer programs like 'Dragon Speak' didn't work because of Evin's trach. Nurses couldn't scribe because it was not part of their job. Evin couldn't dictate a paper onto a recorder because he was unable to create a decent paper in one fell swoop just by talking. Like most students, he had to work on it. Giving a recording to a tutor for typing and getting it back was a hassle. Revising and getting another draft took weeks. It was driving Evin mad."

"When it came to Evin, obviously somebody had to do the typing. The tutors were saying, 'Oh my God, I'll lose my job if I do the typing.' So we had to go around and around about that. Evin was really put out. It was the kind of absurdity that drove Evin to distraction. He began to agitate and storm over it. At times, I ended up scribing for Evin. Finally, the tutoring rules changed. I changed them. Since that time, Evin has really changed. I know because Evin still calls and visits me. I continue to help and advocate for him whenever possible."

"Evin has come to grips with things ... he doesn't have that bitter anger that he once had. He's learned how to relate to people and how to teach them to relate to him. Let's face it - he's different and people have to learn how to talk to him. They have to be unafraid of him and he has pretty well made himself available. He's not somebody to fear. He jokes around about things and people hear him joking around. I think he's grown quite a bit since he's been here. He has goals. He didn't have real goals when he first got here. He's become an amazing young man."

Chapter 27

BELONGING

My Good Friend Kyle

I can never express how grateful I am for the lessons I learned at St. Leo. Not just my academic work which is very important to me, but I'm speaking of all of those unquantifiable lessons that I learned about growing to adulthood. At St. Leo's, with the help of friends, professors and counselors, I went from being a fearful, angry, ambitious, entitled and handicapped child to being a self-directed and empowered man.

I met Kyle Hickman in my 9 a.m. English class. The first day of class, I was sitting next to him and he leaned over and said, "Hi, how are you? My name's Kyle." I immediately thought he wanted something from me. I just wasn't used to strangers being so friendly, so nice to someone like me. We started talking and we hit it off right away. Kyle was in ROTC and was very busy - he only slept about three hours a night. But even though he had so much to do, if I needed anything, he'd find a way to help. One day when I was taking an open-book test in Miss Chris' office and couldn't find my book, he ran all the way across campus and back to bring the book to me. In class, we'd always sit together and sometimes he'd start dozing off and I'd smack the desk with my wheelchair to wake him up. He'd always say if it weren't for me, he wouldn't have gotten straight A's.

Kyle is one of those rare people who is not biased toward anything or anybody. He's the kind of person who is sickeningly optimistic and everything they do, they do it 120 percent. Nothing you say can get them down. Even when Kyle had a bad day, he'd still be smiling. He seemed very content with life in

general …not frenetically happy but very comfortable with himself and very accepting of others. Kyle is the kind of guy that even on your worst day, he makes you feel happy.

After English that semester, Kyle and I always made sure we had at least one class together. I was lucky to have met and made a friend like him. These days, Kyle is in the army. With his ambition and hard work, I have no doubt he will one day end up as a General!

Wearing my Frat Colors

I had a new determination to take advantage of all opportunities and to do anything I could do, not just things I wanted to do. So I decided to try out for power soccer – even though I was seriously skeptical.

Power soccer is one of the few worldwide motorized wheelchair sports. The United States Power Soccer Association (powersoccerusa.org) has worked over the years to standardize rules, play and competitions. The wheelchairs are all custom made, very low – only inches off the ground, kind of like go -carts. The chairs spin faster than regular chairs, with greater Power Soccer momentum. Each chair has bars or a solid guard on the front and sometimes the back. These are used to hit the ball. The ball is 13 inches in diameter - bigger than a regular soccer ball.

There is a team of four players during a game but you have more players on a team altogether. Goalies protect the goal as in regular soccer. The way we played, the chairs were able to hit a ball possibly up to 40 miles an hour given the strength of the chair and how the driver hits the ball. The official rules limit the speed of the chair to 10 mph. I found a local team that was just forming. We called ourselves Phoenix Rising. I loved it and I got very engaged. I bought some equipment plus jerseys for all of our players. We practiced at least once a week and we started to meet at each others' homes to bond better as a team. Playing games and being able to pound the ball was a great outlet.

Fraternity Party at My Place

There were personality conflicts but even that was empowering. I discovered during a practice that I would not be taken advantage of anymore. And as an adult I demanded a certain amount of respect. There was a player on another team who was horribly rude and condescending. Nobody would confront him. His parents let him do whatever he wanted because he was disabled. (Actually, he was able-bodied from the waist up; he could use his arms.) He'd say things like, Get me some f-ing water, bitch!

During a practice game, I was in the wrong spot because I was still learning the rules, and this kid told me to get my f-ing ass over there. Without a word, I rammed my chair full speed into the side of his chair. His chair flew up, teetered and then came back down toward me. I leaned my chair down so our eyes were level and I said, "I'm 24 and you're 17. I'm an adult and you're a child. I don't give a damn about your cripple-ass legs. Talk to me like that again and I will push your ass into oncoming traffic." Then I repeated my new mantra: "You're legs may be disabled but your manners are not."

Some people may think that a physical attack like that was wrong but it was right for me. He never spoke to me like that ever again. I think it was right for that teenager, too. I will never forget that moment as a really big step forward. When you are disabled, you are powerless in so many ways. It is very important to see how you can be empowered … empowered to defend yourself, as well as to behave with courtesy and respect. That was a defining moment for me because I realized that I have a voice. I have a right to be respected – not because of my wheelchair, but because I'm a human being.

Unfortunately, our team did not last. The team was run by the grandfather of a player who had been treated badly by another team. Our able-bodied leader was holding a grudge. He was vengeful and he drove us hard. In his mind we had to dominate! Power soccer became all about hard work and getting back at the other team, not about having fun and working together as a team. After some complaints, he quit. I tried to take the lead but after a few weeks and a few hundred dollars, it fell apart. I still love the game and I may play again someday. What I know for sure is that having the opportunity helped me get where I am today.

Change often comes to me by persisting through failure. After all, if you persist, you haven't failed ... you've only had a setback! One of my greatest failures turned into one of my greatest successes.

My friend Kyle belonged to a fraternity, TKE and he recommended I try to get into it, too. I hadn't even considered a fraternity because I believed the stereotype that they are just about partying and getting into trouble but Kyle convinced me otherwise. He is an extremely motivated young man. He was a true patriot who took ROTC very seriously - a gentleman's gentleman. When Kyle said this was a group that was worth joining, I believed I should give it a try. 'Building better men for a better future' was their motto. I thought that even if I didn't get in, maybe I could learn something - something that could help me progress. I could embrace some aspect of social life that up until this point had eluded me.

The idea was terrifying. I really didn't want to spend a lot of time with people my own age- especially a bunch of guys. I'd been around women most of my life - my mom and my female nurses. The very next week was rush week and there were events taking place the entire week. I forced myself to go to an event. I became so scared that I felt like I wanted to learn to walk just so I could jump out the window and run. But I felt I had to try despite my anxiety. I kept telling myself to stay because this experience could be the door that could lead to something that I had never even imagined.

So the whole week I showed up and conversed with many of the brothers. Sadly, the fraternity rejected me. Kyle told me I got voted down because I had a reputation on campus for being disrespectful to women, impatient, and rude to teachers. And I thought I'd gotten rid of that bad rep from several semesters ago. I had tried for so long to get rid of that person! Kyle fought to convince the

My Frat Brothers

fraternity members that I wasn't that person any more but they weren't buying it. That made me mad. I was so steamed - it was like my blood was boiling. I felt I had to redeem myself. I couldn't let it go. I was not that person anymore.

All throughout that same semester, I went to every person I'd ever come in contact with at St. Leo - females, males, professors, people I had known since I'd come to college. I told them the story and asked if they could email me a letter stating what I was like when I first arrived at St. Leo's and what, in their eyes, I was like now. I learned integrity that semester. I got tons of letters and emails from people saying, 'Yeah you used to be that person, very impatient, rude, uncooperative' ... They told me how I had changed for the better. I am so grateful to those people for helping me.

I thought I didn't care about what others thought of me. I didn't even seem to care what I thought of myself. But of course, I did and I do. Even more importantly, I realized that I actually do have a moral compass. I do have guidelines by which I like to live and want to live. And I realized that if somebody saw that I wasn't living by these moral guidelines, I had to go and prove, not so much to others, but to myself that I am this good person and not a disrespectful jerk.

The next semester I went to try for TKE again. And I brought my emails to prove I was different now. Again, I didn't get in by just one vote. Kyle had

Fraternity Charter Ceremony

told me that some of the brothers were not comfortable with someone like me. I wanted to be optimistic and try not to believe these guys whose motto is building a better man for a better world were making decisions based on my disability. But I'm not one to just accept that I couldn't win them over, so the next semester I tried a third time. And when I went to see if I got in, it was no again. Kyle was so disappointed in his brothers. He told me the brothers who didn't want me were making up lies that

I'd run over my nurses with my wheelchair, and I'd told women to f-k off. Never in my entire life have I told a woman to f-k off! And running a nurse over in my wheelchair was absurd. I knew that not every TKE chapter was like this but this chapter was not living up to its standards. I decided to quit trying.

I was leaving the building where I was told I didn't make it, when suddenly I had this gut feeling that said, 'Turn around and go back right now.' I ended up finding Tom, the man who was in charge of Greek life at St. Leo. I asked him, 'What do I have to do to start my own fraternity?' I had seen this chapter's true colors. I thought would start my own fraternity and show them how men are supposed to conduct themselves.

He said it could be done but it would take a long time. Time for me was running out. I had only two semesters left at St. Leo. I was thinking, this is just a lost cause. All of a sudden Tom said there was a group on campus that was trying to start a new chapter of a fraternity. They had completed the paperwork and they were looking for "founding fathers." The "founding fathers" would be the ones who made up the bylaws, traditions, pledge programs and such, essentially creating the foundation of what our chapter would become. I said enthusiastically, where are they? I met with a man who was from the national organization and was helping to get things started. I was so excited that when I approached him, even before he could say his name, I said: Where do I pay! As I was leaving, I realized I didn't even know the name of the fraternity. He said: "Kappa Sigma."

If I had not heeded that small voice that told me to go back inside - if I had not found Tom right then, I would never have found something that has been a precious source of inspiration and fellowship for me - my fraternity. That night, we met across the street at a restaurant called The Tavern. There were about 25 to 30 guys - they were rambunctious, passionate and crazy! My first thought was: Uh - oh, what did I join?

But I liked it. I enjoyed just sitting there and being a part of it. I began to look forward to any and all events or meetings that we had to attend. One of the first things we did was sit in a big circle for three hours going over our bylaws. After about an hour, people were getting antsy, tired and bored. But to me it was exciting. I was just happy to be there. I thought it was so much fun! After three hours, when it was time to go I was like: Really, we're done? Can't we keep going?

In the next couple of weeks, I discovered some brothers were there because they just wanted the "founding father" credit on a resume. They never showed up for the chapter meetings and events. Some brothers dropped out of school. The rest of us worked for about a year on things like our traditions and tweaking bylaws until we became "colonized". This meant that the national organization acknowledged that we were an actual group even though we didn't yet have a charter. Not having a charter meant we are not yet official members of the fraternity. As I got to know more about our fraternity, I realized my personal values and morals synched up perfectly with Kappa Sigma.

Chapter 28

COMING OUT

Yes, I am Different

It was in one of my psychology classes that I finally came to a deeper understanding of my own sexuality.

One day, my professor had us separate into two groups to debate. The groups were those who believed being gay was a choice and those who thought being gay was not a choice. Because of my many secret struggles with this exact situation, I wanted to sit in the middle and asked if this was possible. The professor chuckled and said. "No, you have to pick a side."

There were 15 students on the side of "It's not a choice" and two students who were very passive and quiet on the side of "It is a choice." Clearly, the debate was going to be a massacre. But I liked a challenge, so I joined the two girls on the side of choice – even though I secretly wanted to be on the other side. After the debate was over, I was changed. After all the years in which I'd dealt with being gay and not knowing whether or not I had control, I realized that I could control my choices. I could control whether I would go out on a date or be intimate with a man or a women - but I could not control my feelings about it. Since I was 13 years old, I felt like I was going crazy because of this. All of a sudden, I realized I was not crazy. My sexuality was not my choice! A huge burden had been lifted.

This realization prompted me to ask people who were straight and thought being gay was a choice to try something. Try going out on a date with someone of your own sex and feel sexually attracted to him or her. Try to force yourself to become sexually aroused. Push yourself to imagine getting undressed with that person and enjoying it. If you are straight, those feelings are just not going to happen. You can't force the feelings. Your sexual feelings are part of who and what you are. I finally came to realize that a personality trait is not a sin. It is something that you're born with and will always be with you. We cannot control the DNA in our bodies. Trying to control being gay is like trying to control how your liver metabolizes food.

After that class in which we debated choice in being gay, I went to my weekly appointment with Aunt Karen, the physical therapist. Aunt Karen has been gay for years and she's also a Christian. (One other person in our family is also gay – more evidence of an inherited trait.) Aunt Karen believes there is nothing in Christian values that prohibits being gay or being in a gay relationship. That day, I came out of the closet. Aunt Karen was the very first one I told. I knew she would understand some of the struggles I had been going through. She was very supportive and helped me stop judging myself so harshly. After that, I started telling other people who were close to me.

The funny thing is, after I came out of the closet, I realized that I am also attracted to women, but in a different way. It's called being "demi-sexual." Someone who is demi-sexual is a person who does not experience sexual attraction based on physical characteristics but may develop a sexual attraction based on an emotional or mental connection. There was a female student at my university who I'd gotten to know on a personal level. I had a crush on her because of who she was, not because of how she looked. Eventually, I started to become attracted to her in a sexual way. My attraction to her physically was based on my attraction to her personality. I realized then that I have a homosexual attraction to men but I have a "demi-sexual" attraction to women. Yes, I am *Different*, I think I've always been "demi-sexual" toward women.

For example, there was a girl at my church that I liked. I'm not going to lie: I had a crush on her. I've always had a crush on her. We met when I was about seven years old and we became friends. She was the first girl I met who looked past my physical differences and could see the real Evin. When others would run off, she would wait up for me. She made me feel happy and safe. Many times after Sunday services I would tell her to hop on the back on my wheelchair to ride around the parking lot!

After coming out of the closet, I got a harsh letter from one of my great religious friends in Tennessee. She had been a really nice older lady who

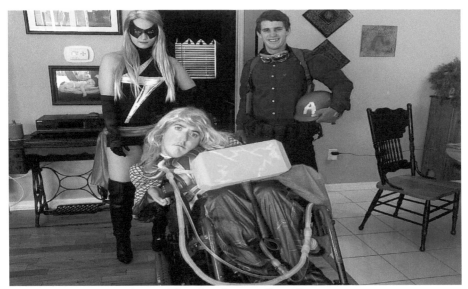

Thor heading to ComiCon

genuinely seemed to always care about how I was doing. The letter was very blunt and felt like an attack. It ended with "Repent or you'll end up in hell."

I discussed the letter with my preacher and an elder in my church. They helped me to understand the harshness of some Christians' judgments. They helped me to see the difference between feelings and actions, lust and love. We as Christians and as a society have taken personality and actions and clumped them together. For example, if a straight married man sees a woman and thinks, "Wow, she's beautiful and attractive," and then moves on, that's not a sin. Our choices are our actions, not our feelings.

Having a personality trait like being gay doesn't mean you have to act upon it. At least for me, I don't choose to travel that path but that might not be the case for others. As a Christian, I choose to not act upon those feelings. I don't judge anybody else, though. What I choose is only what is right for me. I believe it is very important to listen to all points of view.

Uncle Evin

Chapter 29

THE WILL TO LIVE WELL

It took a while but today, I am content. These days, I rarely get depressed. I cannot imagine a life without my disability. Due to my own near-death experiences as well as losing so many friends early in my life, I have accepted death as a part of life. I no longer feel terribly sad if someone I know dies. I'm also not afraid of almost anything because most things we are afraid of can kill us.

Once you are no longer afraid of death, there isn't much left to be afraid of - at least for me. I don't like the word "hope." I prefer the word "will." In my younger years, hope paralyzed me. I hoped I would be cured; I hoped I would someday lead a normal life. To many people, hope can be a powerful thing. But for me, hope caused a crippling depression.

I can't wait for a miracle to happen. I can't hope for opportunities or a great life. What I can do is create a great life for myself. Knowing that a cure may not happen in my lifetime helps me to stop focusing on a life that I may never have - a life without my disability. It helps me to focus on my happiness and success in this life. I don't want to fight who I am anymore. I have already achieved a great deal in this life.

I do, however, every now and then, want things that are not easily achieved because of my disability. For example: children, a girlfriend, a wife, privacy. It sometimes makes me sad that I have tons of female friends but never have been in an intimate relationship.

My life revolves around spirituality. I have done and achieved everything in my life thanks to God. I am an open-minded Christian who truly accepts everyone. I like studying about other religions and lifestyles; I'm willing to accept others regardless of our differences. Just because I believe 100 percent something is wrong doesn't mean I'm right. Who am I to judge you and your beliefs and lifestyles? I can only judge myself and what I want to do with my life. I still love spreading the word of Jesus Christ but I don't want to force anything on anyone. If you don't choose Christianity, I still would love to be friends. Some of my greatest friends are atheists. I don't believe God has punished me by giving me this disability. I feel rewarded with this life I have. Living life with a disability is a great opportunity to see life differently and influence things in a way that not many others can.

In a way, though it sounds odd, sometimes I love being disabled. It's given me so much freedom – which is funny because for most my life, I thought my disability limited my life. But it also opened rare and unique opportunities.

Today, I am going forward with not only my own plans and ideas but also with whatever opportunities open up to me. I got my Bachelor's degree in Psychology but have not yet found a Psychology Masters program that I can attend. Meanwhile, I'm going back at St. Leo's to earn my MBA in business – in marketing, to be precise. Who knows what new avenues will open up for me? Though I never wanted to be a writer, I'm writing this book and planning another one about teaching disability awareness. My goal is to become financially independent from my parents and, someday, to live on my own.

The main thing is that I learned how to accept myself as I am and to feel grateful for every opportunity that comes my way. I learned that I can accomplish almost anything by saying, "I will." If I have anything to teach, it is to believe it is good and right to find your own way toward your goal. Just don't give up or give in. "Failure" is not part of the picture. Just because we fall down on the way toward our goal doesn't mean we've failed. Believe me, a brick wall is just a temporary detour. Don't be afraid to stand up for your rights. Don't be afraid to ask for help. Make a fuss. **Be the storm, be the change, and just say "I Will", and you will find a way to get there from here.**

I'm now committed to help others understand that – 'If You Can't Adapt to the World You Live in, Then Don't! Instead, just Create Your Own World in Which You can Live'. Through my life's experiences, I learned to create a Disabled World, where I am Abled to help it!

My Dad recently shared a saying with me that he had read many years ago and ever since it has helped him through life's struggles. I've learned to understand its meaning and would like to share it with you as well.

"When we cry out for help in the raging Storms of Life, Sometimes GOD Calms the Storm. But Sometimes He lets the Storm continue to Rage and He Calms the Soul".

St. Leo University President presenting Evin's Master Degree Sash

Epilogue

Evin knows what it's like to be Abled in a Disabled World because he lived it. His body was twisted to the visual eye but his spirit and heart were straight as an arrow. He knew how to love and be loved as he shared his gifts with the world. There was never a minute he didn't leap at the chance to sing, clown around, poke fun at you, or test your limits. He was good at pushing boundaries, whether they were personal or societal. Hopefully, you paused for a minute as you read this book to truly capture the essence of Evin's truth.

I'm not really sure what Evin had in mind when he started working on this book project but I can clearly see the value of his efforts. Unless you have a disabled person in your family, you tend not to think about them, and when you see one on the streets or out in public, we tend to stare, or shift our eyes, but never approach them to try for a better understanding. Evin understood this dynamic and it never disturbed or seemed to bother him. He was on a mission to steer society in the right direction with the few days he had on earth. He had the insight for pushing society's buttons that needed to be pushed.

Thank you for entering into Evin's life by reading this book and hopefully getting to know him a little better. It's not possible to read his story without thinking introspectively about your own life and how much we too easily take things for granted. Evin showed us how to live life to its fullest every single day. Even in death, he continues to inspire, encourage, challenge, and remove barriers with his story. Rarely will we ever have the chance to truly touch someone from the inside out as Evin has done in a mighty way with the words on these pages.

This is a seminal work that allows you to see the world from the eyes of a person with muscular dystrophy. It's important to keep your eyes open as you put this book down and start today by making a contribution to those with disabilities so that they too can live life to the fullest. Evin lived his whole life knowing that his days were numbered and that every single event or activity could possibly be his last. I want you to deeply imagine the mental pressures these types of thoughts can cause. Most people in Evin's condition may ask, "Why me?" Evin's story is proof- positive of his response, "Why not me!" Evin realized that he had a divine purpose, and that was to positively influence those around him, and then later in death to change the world.

Are you up to the challenge of making a significant difference in your life? Evin showed us how to live. While he was a youngster, he did not make excuses for his looks or limited capabilities, but used what he had and learned to change the conversation from himself to others. Once in his wheelchair, he liked to go fast! At camp, he was first to participate in every activity. At home, he played hard with his brothers and pushed his parents to realize new boundaries. At school, he refused to accept established norms by creating new standards. What more is possible in your life if you merely leverage Evin's courage to dare? Evin dared us to accept everyone around us. To give them the same opportunities that you desire without passing judgment and to view each person as an equal.

Abled in a Disabled World has a way of bridging the gap between sanity and insanity. Just when you think you'd be ready to throw up your hands and give up, this family finds the fortitude and most importantly, the love on which to rely. Their love conquered all-through the missteps, shortcomings, and oversights. Evin made everyone around him pay close attention to the smallest of things because everything counted! Every second, every event, every activity, every word-everything had to be considered. While most people would be completely fatigued, the Hartsells' could not afford to get exhausted because Evin would not let them. His mission in life was unconditional and he lived it the way it was intended.

The Hartsell family was blessed to provide stewardship for Evin during his brief time on earth and they did a remarkable job. Most days they did not have all the answers but had to rely on their deep faith and trust in God's plan. After reading this book, you experienced the highs and lows of this family and witnessed times where they felt like giving up. Several gut-wrenching near-death experiences are accounted, as well as times both parents felt like pulling their hair out because they did not know what to do! Being a military family has unique challenges on its own merits and meeting the demands of having a handicapped child is doubly taxing. Moving from base to base, forcing the children to change schools was difficult. Securing full time, around the clock medical assistance for Evin was even more challenging. Through it all this family stuck it out by making the best of every situation.

I am honored to play a small part in this project, and realize there are several others who actually knew Evin, and had the chance to witness his brilliance on a daily basis. If you had the opportunity to meet Evin, consider yourself extremely fortunate. Evin may be gone from our eyesight but his legacy lives on in his words. We hope that you cherish and appreciate his experiences and use them to improve your own life and others by becoming Abled in a Disabled World!

~ Dr. Gerald D. Curry, Publisher

First Visit

29th Birthday Remembrance

Personal Reflections

My Son,

Life changed in the blink of an eye

I miss you Son....My heart aches to see you again, to hear your voice one more time, to hear you yell out from your room as I walk in the door "Hello Darlin"!

I miss our EPIC conversations.

I miss our colorful debates...always with love.

I miss your quick wit and warped sense of humor. I miss the out of the box way you looked at life.

I miss your compassion for others and protection of those who you saw as weak, whom you felt needed your strength.

I miss your fierce protection of me, no one, and I mean no one could mess with your Mama or you would pounce without hesitation.

I miss your strength...So much stronger than most I know!

I miss your passion for your beliefs...and your perseverance to fight for those beliefs.

I miss your Faith in me, you truly thought I was unstoppable and there was nothing I couldn't fix or do. You gave me the strength to endure things I never thought possible Son.

You taught me patience Son, patience for myself and others... Oh, how you had an abundance of patience!

I miss you singing! Always singing!!! Made me smile from the other side of the house and brought me such joy! You endured so much Son.... Emotional and physical pain and you did it with such grace, some spiciness and a whole lot of stubbornness.

I miss your Love, Son! I miss my friend!

I called you My Compass Evin and without you, I feel lost.

Because I Can Son, I will get your story out to the world. I will be your voice and people will know the incredible young man I loved for 28 years. I know they will be inspired as I was for all those years.

I am so fortunate and lucky God gave me you to care for, I only hope I blessed you as much as you blessed me.

~ MOM

The day after Evin passed from this Life, Melisa and I, our son Alex and his wife Lindsey, our son Nathan, and my sister Karen were all gathered together in our home, and we were all talking about our fondest memories of Evin and how he inspired each and every one of us, as well as so many others throughout his life. I listened to what everyone was saying and asked everyone to think of a word or a character trait that best described who and what Evin was to them and this is the list we came up with;

Persistence

Endurance

Patience

Stubborn with a Strong Will to Succeed

Giving

Supportive Heart Healer

Competitive

Master of Verbal Engagement

Humorous – Wit with Grit

Bluntness with Honesty – with the intent to get to a Solution

Leadership

Inspiration for All

~ *Dad*

I first met Evin in the fall of 2016 when he came to my office for a "verbal engagement" to discuss his interest in joining a fraternity. Evin was not a Criminal Justice major and I was unsure of his reason for coming to see me, but I found out rather quickly. As it turned out, Evin had not had a good experience in Greek rush and our fraternity was in the process of colonizing at Saint Leo University and he had determined that he wanted to become a Kappa Sigma. Thus, began a friendship that grew and strengthened over the next 21 months. Evin became a charter initiate of the chapter and our friendship and mutual respect for each other strengthened as we had numerous "verbal engagements" and conversations on a variety of issues – university policies and procedures, fraternity policies and procedures and life in general. My lasting memory of Evin will be of him at the chapter's anniversary party at his home. He was so proud and happy as the members of the chapter gathered together to celebrate their the anniversary of the chartering and the end of the term at Saint Leo.

Evin was a man of keen insight and great potential that was taken from us much too early. He touched me deeply, as he touched many people at Saint Leo, in Kappa Sigma and in society in general. He was my friend and brother and I am grateful for the time we had together, and I miss him.

Semper,
~ *David Persky, Ph.D., J.D.*
Past Worthy Grand Master, Kappa Sigma Fraternity
Professor of Criminal Justice, Saint Leo University

Dear Evin,

Thank you for your openness and your honesty. With so many people that I talk to and counsel, its like pulling teeth to know what they actually think, feel, struggle with, fear, hate, love. While I am not so arrogant as to believe you told me every detail and secret you had, it was an honor to be trusted with even some of them. Which, of course, allowed me the safety to share some of mine. Thank you. Granted, sometimes your honesty and openness were a little frightening. But I believe we need more of that kind of honesty among brothers. I appreciate yours.

And to top it all off, thanks for sharing Taco Tuesdays with me. I wish now I had cleared my schedule for that more often.

I miss you. But I look forward by the grace of Jesus to seeing you again.

Thanks,

~ *Edwin L. Crozier (Church family friend and Preacher)*

When I was younger Evin took my family and I to light fireworks. Turns out we were strapping Barbie dolls to the fireworks and we ended up setting a field on fire...I love you Evin, you had such an impact on my life and you're the reason I'm the person I am today.

~ *Payton (Nurse's daughter)*

I first met Evin at MDA Summer Camp when he was 5 years old and ran over my foot with his electric wheel chair, which by the way was the smallest electric wheel chair I had ever seen. I did not realize at the time that he had not only ran over my foot but that he had driven straight into my heart and my life would never be the same again. I had the privilege of watching Evin grow from a cute little boy with a huge smile to an adult with a wicked sense of humor but the one thing that never changed was his love and compassion for others. From the time that Evin was just a child he could not stand to see someone upset or what he considered being left out and would go out of his way to talk to them. Evin loved people and he had that special ability to make you feel like you were the only one in the world that matter. Evin loved being the center of attention and especially the attention of the ladies which he got all the time. One of my favorite memories of Evin took place during his last year at camp and involved his camp picture.

We had a tradition of framing and presenting the kids pictures of camp and for one of these pictures they got to pick out who they wanted to be in the picture with them. Most of the kids picked out a few close friends but leave it up to Evin to ask every female from camp to be in the picture with him and then he didn't want anyone to feel left out so he asked the male counselors and campers to be in the picture with him. By the time the picture was actually taken I think he had the entire camp, which I loved because it represented the Evin I knew and loved. I am so thankful that Evin chose to share his love of life and his love of people with me and my life were greatly enriched because of this.

~ *Betty S. (MDA Camp Counsellor)*

You've officially infiltrated my mind, Evin! Believe it or not, sweet memories of our time together flood my heart on the regular. Whether I'm stumbling upon an episode of Friends, working on a complex puzzle, passing by a casino, spinning circles at the skating rink, munching on some Oreos (especially the golden ones), using an electric toothbrush, etc. I am always having your crazy self pop up in my mind. Seriously, though, I couldn't have asked for a better person to show me the ropes on how to care for someone with a trach and ventilator.

I was always amazed at how in-tune you were with your body and at your confidence to make decisions that weren't necessarily by the book. And I love that if you could do this thing, called life, all over again, that you wouldn't have changed a thing; because your unique journey helped form you into the unstoppable force you became. I truly wish I could've seen you have your own little kiddos. I can just imagine all the entertaining conversations my boys would've had with their Uncle Evin. Sadly (for us), those hilarious conversations will have to be postponed for a while. Looking forward to seeing you again, brother. Love you always.

~ *Corey (Nurse)*

Evin will always have a special place in my heart and it will always be an honor to call him my nephew. I will never forget his kisses, his smile, his laughter, his big blue eyes, his singing and his passion to excel and overcome. His Uncle Ron and I loved him dearly. One of the photos I cherish is from our wedding day and Melisa was expecting him. We would get to meet him 3 months later and he was a special gift. I will miss the love he had for his parents and his brothers and the love they had for him. I still miss him and the family times with him. My prayers are with Melisa, Scott, Alex and Nathan.

~ Aunt Cindy

To My Honey Lamb, Evin. From your sugar lips, Nana.

I miss you so much Evin. I find myself talking to your picture on the wall and thinking about our time together. I look at you and smile and know I can't wish you back because of the pain you were in, you never complained and I was so amazed at how strong you were. We had a special relationship of pestering one another but always in love. I loved to kiss your cheeks with lipstick on and you would roll away like you didn't like it but I know you did. It was a joy to my heart when you started calling me sugar lips and I called you my honey lamb. I will always miss you and keep you forever in my heart. May God bless and keep our families.

~ Your Sugar Lips AKA Nana (Grandmother)

To me Evin was normal. With the exception of a few physical differences, Evin was just like both of my other nephews! When people met EVIN, they quickly learned to not feel sorry for him, and most actually would envy him for his no filter,...no boundary take on life! Sometimes hysterical, sometimes shocking, but always the truth, and always EVIN! I'm so thankful that EVIN and I had very special and close bond and that he was able to confide in me when he needed an ear about many things (sincere and funny). Evin discussed some of these topics in his book, but there were many other memories/experiences that we experienced together that permanently and positively impacted my day to day take on life.

Evin taught me to live in the moment and make life fun when possible! Evin never took anything too seriously and thought that it was ok at times to bend the truth a little as long as no one got hurt and no 'specific' laws were broken. One example of this viewpoint, was when Evin and his nurse would frequently drive up for Physical Therapy treatments (although his appointment mostly consisted of me stretching him while we gossiped and often debated about current world topic).

On one our scheduled stretching/gossip appointments, he and his nurse (who was driving) were running behind and got pulled over by the FHP for speeding. EVIN had a trick where he could hold his breath which would trigger a loud obnoxious ventilator alarm noise. So as a diversion and as the trooper walked up to the car EVIN started shaking his head and body like he was feigning a seizure which triggered his vent alarm. Obviously the officer went from a possible speeding violation mode into potential emergency mode at about the same that time that Evin suddenly began immediately recovering and explained to the officer (between gasps) that his nurse had been driving fast to get him to his Aunt Karen's medical office because he was worried. Yeah, no ticket, and although so wrong on so many levels, very hysterical and very Evin! Evin always claimed that he WAS actually going to my office so part of his act was true!

Evin always had a get 'er done attitude! EVIN called me in 2017, to tell me he volunteered to head the decoration committee for one of his fraternity induction parties. He said he knew he was the only one who had an aunt with horses, and thought that I could bring him 50 bales of hay. The only problem was that they had a $50.00 budget. Unfortunately, I had to inform him that the actual cost and logistics wouldn't support his initial plan, so instead through some discussion and compromise we were able to come up with the solution of five bales and rope for barriers and other barn theme appropriate decorations that were well within his budget. Problem solved!

Evin lived competitively and taught that patience is good! From a young age, Evin's competitiveness was displayed overtly and often whether it was with his brothers in video marathons, with other athletes during power soccer practices, with other students during classroom debates, and also with himself! One example of his competitiveness with himself was when he was visiting me in Ocala and he had me time 'laps' from my gate down my long driveway around the circle drive and back over and over and over for hours on end. He was determined to beat each 'best' time and most of the time, he did! My lesson was patience!

Evin WAS a normal guy and wanted to be looked upon as any other college student! When EVIN turned 21, he called me to ask if I would take him out for his first drink, so I took him to Bubba Gumps' restaurant. He boldly ordered a Bushwhacker from the waiter who seemed a little unsure and immediately looked at me so I said "I think you better card him to check his age because I cant remember his birthdate". Evin with the biggest beautiful grin on his face and immediately said "grab my wallet in the side pocket of my chair buddy!" I suddenly realized he didn't really care about the drink at all, he just wanted the experience of being carded like everyone other 21 year old! I'll never forget that look on his face that said MISSION ACCOMPLISHED!

Evin had many mission accomplished moments in his 28 ½ years and I feel blessed to have been able to have been present for many of EVIN's milestones! His academic accomplishments, his battles against big insurance companies for his right to appropriate care, the many major surgical procedures he endured, and the ever present daily battles to live and function in a world not designed for him was nothing short of amazing and just examples of his never ending determination and WILL! Yes, Evin did have frustrations from time to time but his mantra truly was that the world needed to change and WOULD change to accommodate him. Not visa-versa! His perseverance during all of these battles never ceased to amaze me! I frequently remind myself of his many 'missions' whenever I think a task it too daunting.

I feel so lucky to have had the opportunity to have been this awesome dude's aunt, because our many funny and crazy experiences will always live on in my memory and in my heart. Even though Evin depended on family, nurses, and friends to help him simply live (breathe, eat, move, bathe, etc…) on a daily basis, I think all have realized since his loss how much we actually depended on him! He truly reminded us (often verbally) and everyone he encountered to keep things in perspective and appreciate little things we frequently take for granted! Evin didn't have the luxury of taking ANYTHING for granted and he appreciated every second of his life as demonstrated by his actions, his beautiful singing voice, and his devotion and desire to protect those he loved.

I loved this kid (man) beyond measure! He will always be my sexy little nephew, and I will always be his crazy aunt K!

~ *Karen Hartsell (Aunt Karen)*

Evin,
Although I only met you once, I feel like I've always known you through the love and stories shared by your mom, my lifelong friend. What a truly remarkable life you had – I will always remember your tenacity and spirit.

Much Love Hartsell's - I love you all so Much

~ *Karen Hawver (Family friend)*

Evin Hartsell was a kind, gentle, beautiful soul who was an inspiration to many. No matter what life threw at him he always seemed to look at the good in all his trials and tribulations and live his life to the fullest. The first time I met Evin he told me I didn't know how to give a proper shower, one thing about Evin is that you always knew where you stood with him! Evin could definitely be a handful, but he was one of the most loyal, loving, accomplished, fun, exceptional people I've ever had the honor and privilege to call my friend. I will miss you the rest of my days buddy!

~ Sarah Cooke, (Caregiver and family friend)

Evin, Where do I even begin…We have shared so many memories over the years. It's crazy to see how we grew since first meeting you. I remember every time I would walk into your house you would yell "Megan" and you would always know it was me, You could somehow see me before I could see you. I will miss our long conversations that simply stared with just "hey Evin"! You were like a brother to me. You made me realize things about myself I didn't even know. I will miss your laugh, smile, and kind loving spirit. All of my memories with you will not fit on this paper…too many…I love you Evin

~ Megan (Family friend)

Evin,
I still can't believe the news. You changed my life and the lives of so many around you. Your love and passion and unwillingness to settle drew me in from the moment we met. Not once did I ever see you as being unable to do what you set your mind to, and for those who did, you moved mountains to prove them wrong. Your voice, your attitude, your bluntness, your humor, you whole view on life itself made those with closed minds uncomfortable, but that's exactly what they needed, whether they knew it or not.

I will never forget the long conversations we would have on the phone about life, God, love... the laughs we shared, the music video we had to make, the talks that turned into debates.... Everything with you was always nothing short of purity and honesty. You always used to say that you liked me because I never treated you like you were different. That always stuck with me, not because it made me feel special, but because you never realized how truly beyond this world you really were. You were truly abled in a disabled world. You had big dreams and an even bigger heart. You knew how to love and how to be a true friend, you knew that life wasn't about your struggles, but about educating, speaking out for those who felt like they couldn't, and most importantly making difference.

You had so much going for you, Evin. It saddens me that you will never teach that class, that you won't physically be here to see your book released, that you won't get to be here to continue your work yourself... Just know, good friend, you changed many lives in your short time here. Kyle and I have always known the power in your words and I feel confident in saying that we will never let you memory or your hard work die.

You will always have a special place in my heart, Evin. I will always remember how we used to joke and how you would nonchalantly profess your love to me. Most importantly, I will always remember your fight, your passion for love, life, and your fraternity, your love of God, and your ability to do and thrive in a world that is really the disabled one. I will take you with me for the rest of my life. I know you are happy now watching us from above. Rest easy, my friend. Until we meet again.

~ Lola Manley (College friend)

Evin,

I loved coming to visit you at your house and so many times we would gather around the kitchen table and play games. You loved playing games and one in particular was a game called "Never Trust A Pirate" from the movie Pirates of the Caribbean. It was a game based on deception and you loved the competition and deception. I loved those times and love and miss you.

~ Your Poppy (Grandfather)

On April 28, 2018, I lost someone who was not only a Brother, but one of my Best Friends. Evin Hartsell was an amazing influence in my life. Evin's tenacious attitude and love of Kappa Sigma inspired me to achieve the two ritual proficiency levels I have. I promised Evin I would get at least one more level and I plan to live out that promise. Evin will always be one of my closest friends. To all the people who knew Evin, I hope he touched your heart like he did mine. I know he is at peace now and I send my prayers to Evin's family and anyone else who is mourning after the loss of a True Gentleman and a lawful Kappa Sigma. AEKDB, Evin. AEKDB!

~ Tyler Davis (Fraternity brother)

Evin,

I still can't believe the news man, you had so much going for you and it hurts to know you won't physically be here to see it all.

To some you were just a loud dude in a wheelchair they would never think about approaching, to others like Lola, Cody, and I you were a giant in a human body. I'll never forget the first time we met in Dr. Marino's class at Saint Leo, I was nervous and had no idea of what to do or say to you. I never thought in a million years the friendship we formed would have resulted from a simple conversation. A conversation so many people are apprehensive about having.

Evin you made it clear to everyone that you would not accept mediocrity, that in a world surrounded with complacency you would never give up the fight. You taught me what it means to truly be able in a disabled world. You showed me that friendship has no boundaries. Most importantly though, you inspired me to be a better person and to not take what I have for granted.

Your never quit mentality showed in every conversation you had with others. Your sometimes blunt and seemingly abrasive style was exactly what you needed to get people's attention, and when they wouldn't listen, you got louder.

You sent me a text on Monday asking to give you a call when I could. I never made that call, and now I'll never be able to call you again. I promise you Evin, I promise that I will never regret not making a phone call to someone like I do right now, ever again. I will continue to use our friendship as an example to live by in my future. Although you are gone physically, I will not allow you to be forgotten. You will live on in my thoughts, prayers, and actions for years to come.

Thank you for being the voice representing a population of people who are typically soft spoken and all too often overlooked by society. I can't wait to read your book and see all of the great change you will continue to impart on the world from Heaven because I know you're not done yet. Rest In Peace old friend, I'll see you soon.

"As iron sharpens iron, so one person sharpens another."

Proverbs 27:17

~ Kyle Hickman (College friend)

Evin,

I will always remember how you pushed my damn buttons! More than that, I will always remember how quick you were to apologize, and never afraid to ask for forgiveness from those you loved. I wish I had responded to your last message but I know you are with me in my trying times. I love you and I'll always remember us!

~ *Jessica (Your first nurse in Florida)*

My earliest standout memory of Evin Hartsell, 2 words, purple wig! It was a Halloween party and as usual, Evin was having a blast. He was wheeling around in his wheelchair like a Nascar driver, smiling, laughing, cracking jokes, and talking to everyone! This was Evin, full of life. That love of life and his accomplishments never ceased to amaze me. This " what can I do to make things better" is my greatest memory and inspiration from Evin.

Thank you Evin !

~ *Mitzi Ware (Family friend)*

Where to start. That is the question? I asked Evin that during our time together. His answer was, *At the beginning.*

I became acquainted with Evin in his late teens when the progression of his disease resulted in him being placed on a ventilator. I was assigned to care for him as part of a 24/7 team of nurses. To make a long story short, he was not a happy camper. He told me back then he couldnt kick my ass with his hands but he could with his words. I remember thinking to myself, what have I gotten myself into! I continued to assist with providing care for him until one day he said he was done with me.

I was assigned to another client but it became evident that he did not want to get rid of me. The agency called and told me he said he was just joking. LOL By that time I had already become established with another client. A few years passed and I was offered the opportunity to assist again with his care. I agreed because I believe that assumptions can more times than not be inaccurate. I like the saying, *"Contempt Before Investigation"* does no one any good. So, when I arrived to meet evin, I was cautiously optimistic. What I found was a young man who, through his own pain and suffering, found peace by helping others.

One example comes to mind. I don't think I can remember the name but I know who it is. It was an girl at SLU who helped out in the guidance counselor's office. She supposedly had some type of nervous twitch and talked alot (which I can relate to the latter, btw). When he was either waiting for something or finished at the guidance counselor's office, he would strike up a conversation with her. He would ask her a question and she would always give him the long version of the answer. I knew what he was up to. The beauty was to watch Evin, who could have justifiably conceded to addressing his own needs, reach out to someone while he thought no one was watching, provide comfort by simply listening and engaging in conversation. In stark contrast to the Evin I met ten or so years earlier who would have said or done God knows what.

So, if you can take anything away from reading this book, remember this; When you help another, in the end, you help yourself. Is it selfish to be helpful to help yourself? I don't know. I do know thats how it winds up in the end though. I have to add in closing that Evin was a product of his environment. He through his short time here carried on what was given to him. The love and support his parents and extended family provided gave him the opportunity to blossom into the loving person he had become in spite of. Hopefully this book will inspire you to trudge on and be an inspiration to someone to live life to its' fullest in spite of lifes' challenges.

~ Louis Feldman (Nurse)

Evin never had an unfriendly or tentative word with me. He was so forthright, genuine and exuded the persona of...."Be Comfortable With Me" I am normal too!" That was a wonderful gift in his condition. Thank you for the lessons your whole family taught us through his life.

~ Marilyn Payne (Church family friend)

The word tenacious has Latin roots. The meaning is: persistent in seeking something valued or desired, holding firmly, forceful. When used figuratively, we would say "stick-to-itiveness". For anyone who had the opportunity to be with Evin Hartsell for any length of time, you left his presence sure that you had met the meaning of tenacious in real life form.

Evin was, simply put, a determined spirit. From his earliest years we watched him overcome one obstacle after another. He gave persistent diligence to anything he set his mind to. To him, any barrier in life just proved to be one more hurdle to leap over and past. He refused to be prohibited from moving forward in his endeavors. He was strong willed to the core.

Evin was courageous and tough. He was frustrated by those who "could" but "didn't ". He expressed his disapproval of people who were physically able to accomplish much in life but chose to throw away opportunity. He was tough enough to fight. Although he was not able to fight physically, he could use his tongue like a sword to battle for things meaningful to him.

Evin used his intellect to overcome his physical limitations. His brain was in constant motion. He pondered, he reflected, he examined, he scrutinized. There were sometimes late night, deep discussions with family members over psychological introspection. He questioned and he did not relent until he received an answer. If you were lucky enough to experience one of these deep discussions, you most likely walked away wondering if you had just been psychoanalyzed as one of his case studies. He was a master at getting a person to divulge their true feelings.

Evin was funny and had a great sense of humor. He loved being the center of attention. He used his wit to his advantage and as a teaching tool when necessary. There was an occasion in which he overheard a conversation between a mother and her young son. The boy was giving his mother a hard time and Evin did not like the attitude he displayed. Evin decided that an intervention needed to take place. When the boy was away from his mother (momentarily) he wheeled up to this young man and quietly disclosed to him that if he "did not eat his vegetables he would grow up to be just like him, in a wheelchair". He promptly put the chair in reverse and wheeled away leaving the young boy bug eyed and terrified. Evin was use to taking matters into his own hands and this situation was no different.

Finally, and most importantly, Evin was lovable. As a family we were privileged to see the tender side of him. He had a heart that wanted to help others. He had a heart that wanted to make a difference in the world. Because of the example we saw in his determined spirit, sense of humor, and his ability to challenge each of us in his own unique way, we can truly say "because we knew him we have been changed for good".

~ *Rusty, Cassy, Kaleigh and Hayden (Beloved uncle, aunt and cousins)*

When I was in elementary school I would always hang out with Evin after school and he would always tease me and give me a hard time by telling me I had to give him a password to walk by him and he decided the passwords would be "Evin Walks"…and for some reason it crosses my mind and never fails to make me laugh.

~ *Sayla (Nurse's daughter)*

When I first think about what friendship means I think of loyalty, honesty and trustworthiness. Evin was so much more than that; he was encouraging, motivational, inspiring and exemplified unconditional love. He was my best friend. We fought like an old married couple most the time but there was no one I trusted more with my heart, my secrets and my life. My favorite memories were spending the night together and having movie marathons. He loved showing me every movie that I had never seen and I loved getting to spend that time with him. He taught me how to find the strength inside myself, how to stand up for myself and that it's ok not to be ok sometimes. He taught me how to be myself without limitations and how to be open and honest without being scared. He called me his Cleopatra and showed me my self-worth. He was my confidant, my teacher, my brother, my rock and one of the most important people in my life. His influence and example will never be forgotten. I love you Evin and I know you are now dancing amongst the stars. Till we meet again my dear friend.

"The best kind of people are the ones that come into your life, and make you see the sun where you once saw clouds. The people that believe in you so much, you start to believe in you too. The people that love you, simply for being you. The once in a lifetime kind of people."

~ *Kate Lattey (College friend)*

I never knew in August 1996, my life would be affected by this big blue eyed, energetic, talented, and smart little boy named Evin Bradford Hartsell. This little fireball taught me how to love and be loved beyond what I could image a student could. Our connection and bond grew stronger each year. I no longer look at Evin as a student. He was my child and we loved each other as such. I am so grateful and blessed that God allowed our paths to cross. I'm more grateful that his parents (Scott and Melisa) shared him with me. Evin taught me how to look beyond my limitations and obtain my goals. Lastly, he taught me how to learn the books of the Bible with and angelic voice.

Love you from Earth to Heaven,
~ *Katricia Hampton (School Assistant)*

Evin-

I no longer have anyone to debate with

And I miss you for that

I no longer have anyone who pops in

and just talks about things

And I miss you for that

I no longer have anyone who needs help

with essay exams or writing papers

And I miss you for that, too

My student, my confidant, my friend

I miss you for everything we shared.

I know you are running and jumping and making fun

Of all of us here – and I'm happy for you

But I still miss you!

~ *Shawn (Nurse)*

Evin,

From the first day I met you, I knew you were special. You had such a great sense of humor and your sarcasm always made me laugh! I thought to myself multiple times during the time I knew you and wondered how someone who had so much potential handled your situation. And when we talked, I knew. You did not let your wheelchair define you. You always reached further than most people your age. Achieving higher education and finding a dream worth fighting for was what I remember. Your nephews were the light of your life and they had a great uncle in you.

One of my favorite things about you was when you would try to run me over with your wheelchair EVERY time I would see you! Our conversations of all your fun hairstyles from your blonde tips to your man bun were always a hot topic. The way you would bat your eyes brings a smile to even now as I think of you doing that.

The one comfort I have now that you are not here to debate with is that you obeyed God's word and now have a home in heaven with Him! I look forward to being with you one day, my friend so we can continue the wonderful friendship we started. Until then, I keep the vision of you walking and leaping and praising God and no longer bound to your wheelchair.

Love you!
~ *Miss Kim (Church family friend)*

When I first met Evin Hartsell I thought to myself, how sad it is to be in his situation, however in getting to know him I realized he had such a spirit and fire that nothing could hold that part of him back!

He loved getting his hair done. I smile when I remember Evin racing down the salon hall in his wheelchair excited about his appointment with me because he loved trying new things with his hair!

We even had to improvise rinsing over a bucket because the sink posed a challenge, We packed towels all over him, but even as the water ran down his face, up his nose and on the floor, he would giggle and make jokes.

Evin has changed so much my perspective on living life with all of it's challenges without even realizing it.

I think about him often and I am so grateful this was his gift he gave to me

~ Karen Turner (Hair Dresser)

One Sunday morning while I was standing in the back of the church building waiting for my kids to get out of Bible class, I heard an unusual noise. It sounded like a coffee machine percolating while a jet engine was revving it's engine to take off mixed with alarm bells ringing. My mind raced with excitement to go and find out what this noisy contraption was…When I turned the corner with my eyes wide open…I saw a family all huddled around this wheelchair that was making all this uncontrollable noise. The mom and dad were pressing buttons, adjusting tubes and then in an instant, it went silent and the parents stood back up like this is was a normal routine. After the dust settled, my eyes were fixed on a frail framed young man sitting in this machine with the biggest smile on his face. I moved closer to the wheelchair in hopes of meeting this young man. Well, this was a loud beginning of a friendship with my "backseat pew buddy" Evin. This is how our family met and sat at church. ..with our pew buddy, Evin.

Over the years we got to watch Evin turn perceived limits into unlimited opportunities. He showed all of us who had the privilege of knowing him and loving him what it meant to be brave and courageous…what it meant to have faith that can move mountains and what it means to look at life through a different lens. He taught my family that we are all physically different but we all share the same human spirit. He lived beyond what some may see as physical or societal limits created by living with a neuromuscular disease…He had no limits and knew strength is more than muscle.

The stark truth is that unless you spend time in a wheelchair, it's impossible to know how it affects every aspect of your life. I realized Evin was teaching me to keep my problems in perspective and to look at every circumstance through his lens of life...No matter how hard, difficult, or insignificant as an opportunity for learning, loving, and shinning Jesus light to others. Evin's triumphant story tells the impact a person can make in the life of another is insurmountable. Thank you Evin for the lesson.
In sisterly Love,

~ Shannon Wagner and Family (Church family friend)

Determined, fun, and a young man with an infectious smile. Evin had an impact on my life I will never forget. Even tough he was confined to a wheelchair, you soon learned it was his way to get where he wanted to go and it did not define him. He got more done than most of us who have the use of our legs and tend to take our mobility for granted. He and I shared a love for Disney and met at the park on one occasion. It was so gratifying and exhilarating to see the park from his perspective. I was involved in an accident four and a half years before Evin died. I had fractured my pelvis and had to learn to walk again. I thought of you so many times, Evin, as I was going through rehab and in a wheelchair. I thought if you and your determination to make things better for yourself and other in your situation. You encouraged me to do the same. I chose to be determined, to have fun and keep smiling. Thank you, Evin! You will always have a special place in my heart.

~ Becky Cawthon (Church friend)

When I first met Evin and his family, my immediate thought was how incredibly welcoming they were to me. As soon as I walked in the door, I could feel the warmth and love radiating from their home. What sticks in my mind about Evin the most is his sense of humor. Evin had a cocky, sarcastic personality that somehow only made him more lovable and charming.

Evin was like an older brother to my son Colin and my daughter Madeline. He was always encouraging me to bring them for a visit, and including them in our activities. They tell me they most remember him taking them for rides on the back of his chair, doing donuts in the parking lot and going to Disney with him.

Evin and I were always on the go; we went out for things like dinner and movies, and I went to class with him sometimes and helped him write papers for school. One of my favorite trips though was a particular trip to Disney. After being there for many hours, his ventilator battery was dying and I said it was time to leave because the back up was in the van way out in the parking lot. Evin insisted he would be just fine, gave me a lecture about how he did not "need" it for oxygen but only to support his breathing, and we stayed for at least another hour before heading home despite my better judgment. I think I earned some gray hair that day! The thing about Evin was, he would never accept the word no, and his will was always stronger.

Evin love to watch comedies, movies such as *White Chicks* and *The Devil Wears Prada* were favorites. And boy did we watch a lot of *Family Guy*. He was the master at split screen, playing video games on one side of the screen while watching a movie on the other.

Though always full of love with a side of snark, the thing most impressive about Evin was his dauntless freedom of spirit. He lived fully, worked hard and played hard, and it was my honor to have known him. He will always hold a special place in my heart and I will think of him often until I see him again one day.

~ Damita (Nurse)

I have so many memories with Evin. None of them are very profound, but all of them are something I will always remember. I remember when we, my parents, brother, and sister drove our big green conversion van to some other state to pick up the boys to stay at our house while Scott and Melisa were away. I remember racing Evin down the streets in Florida trying to beat him or not get run over by him. I remember my sister riding on his power wheelchair as he went as fast as he could go without her falling off. I remember our trip to Memphis and doing whatever it was that kids do. I remember our family trip to the Ozarks and ALL of us hiking the trails with my dad and Uncle Scott carrying Evin in a "mom-made" canvas cloth sling. I remember living in Florida, not loving life, and going to the Hartsell house, my home away from home and finding some peace. I would crash there, eat home cooked food, swim, watch movies, hang out with Evin as we talked about boys, girls, and our general dislike for humans. The point is, I remember, and I'll never forget. No one particular event stands out, but every little meeting, conversation, sideways look, and dirty joke will make me miss him until I see him again. He was my family, my friend, my brother. I love you Evin Hartsell.

~ Shannon (Cousin and friend)

The first time some of us met Evin was at MDA summer camp. He was such a spirited young man who enjoyed various activities such as swimming, arts & crafts, racing his chair, and of course meal times (which included doing the "Hokey Pokey").

My first personal encounter with Evin was after he had injured his foot. He was apparently maneuvering his wheelchair at a high rate of speed in the cafeteria and smashed into a stack of chairs. I distinctly remember during the encounter how extraordinarily polite this young man was…and his mannerisms and sense of humor were unlike most others.

While getting him patched up, we began to converse about various things regarding camp, his family, school, girls, etc. I vividly remember him telling me about his family, because he absolutely lit up. Throughout the rest of that camp week while evaluating his racing wounds, Evin would continually tell me and others about funny things he and his brothers have done in the past. A few months later I had the pleasure of meeting his family, and Evin was certainly the one to introduce us.

Throughout many years, I had the honor of watching Evin grow and develop into a very intelligent man. Evin was a true warrior and overcame many obsticals in his life; in unbelievable ways. Throughout it all he was always polite, respectful, funny, kind to others, which is evident of his true character and the way in which he was raised. Evin loved God, loved his family & friends, and loved to compete in various things…like beating others in chess and playing soccer. Evin had a wonderful sense of humor and was always a pleasure to be around.

I'm very proud and honored to have known this extraordinary man and will always call him my friend…….Fly high my brother. Until we meet again.

(Slow it Down)!

Honorably & Respectfully,

~ *B.G. (Trey) Brasell*, III - RN *(Family friend)*

We have some great memories with Evin and family! When the boys were much younger, they came and stayed with us for a few days so Scott and Melisa could get away. Bill built a ramp up our front steps so Evin's wheelchair could get in the house and we would carry him upstairs to the game room and he and the kids had a great time.... Later we took a joint vacation with their family to the 'wilderness' that was Arkansas. At least Evin viewed the woods/fields/caves that we observed and traversed as wilderness. He had not had the opportunity to explore the outdoors with his power wheelchair having it's 'offroad' limits, so we made a travois type of a chair that Scott and Bill carried Evin in after his wheelchair had gone as far as it could. (It was still there sitting in the middle of the forest when we returned!)

Evin was not real sure of the safety and comfort of this new mode of transportation, but endured like a champ and had some new and unparalleled experiences climbing into bat caves and wandering about in his primitive transport. When the Hartsell family moved to Florida, and Shannon and Zach went to college down there, we spent a good bit of time availing ourselves of their hospitality. We would sit and visit with Evin, and discuss/debate about whatever was on his radar at present. He attended the same college as Shannon and Zach at one point, and was very vocal on encouraging them to assess and upgrade their access, support and accommodations for those like him.

He was very articulate and passionate and had a genuine interest in people as individuals, though people at large often frustrated him. He would be my running escort when I would go out for a jog in the neighborhood, pacing me in the power chair. Evin viewed life as something to approach full steam ahead, something to relish and conquer. He did not let his physical limitations hinder his enjoyment of life, or his passion for his family, friends, and caregivers, which was notable; for debate, for wrestling and for travel, especially to MD camp in Tennessee where he had so many friends and great memories. We love and miss him but know that he has gone beyond this present wilderness of concrete and traffic, of conflict, barriers and ignorance, of pain and suffering, and he rests easy with his God in the promised land.

~ *Bill and Susan Moore (Cousins)*

Our Evin is a bit different than others' Evin. From the first time we met at the MDA telethon at the Peabody Hotel in Memphis, Tennessee, Evin (around 16) was on a mission to mold Gavin (3) into the best version of themselves. The bond was immediate and remarkable. Two very independently unique individuals, yet one at the same time. Although not twins, I suspect the bond was similar maybe even deeper.

Not only did they share a diagnosis, they shared many other similarities. Some of their core traits were the same. They both shared a love of singing, talking, and being in the middle of whatever was going on at any given time. Both seemed particularly fond of beautiful girls. They also shared a unique ability to drive their favorite MDA camp counselors crazy while stealing their hearts.

Another similarity was their love of speed. Which leads to one of our favorite Evin and Gavin memories. Its not the simplest task to get two wheelchair bound, morning hating boys to Disney World for a day together. We had accomplished getting to the park and the boys out of the vehicles before nine a.m. They, of course, decided to race through the parking lot to the park entrance. Evin's chair was a bit faster, so Gavin did the only logical thing an eight year old, NASCAR loving boy would do. He rammed him. They both thought it was hysterical the first few times. Until…Gavin's footrest hooked Evin's ventilator battery cord and shredded it. We hadn't even made it in the park! Evin assured everyone he would be fine. A couple times during the day we would stop and plug into a power source for a little extra breathing help. Although Evin was exhausted by the end of the day, the two of them successfully terrorized a park full of tourists all while making them fall in love with the sight of these two remarkable humans.

Gavin and Evin talked on the phone often. We were fortunate enough to get to visit in person multiple times although there were States between us. Their discussions were often Evin giving Gavin advice on how to handle normal life issues and the issues they faced because of their disease. It was always evident that Evin saw himself in Gavin and vice versa. Evin strived to make Gavin better. It was if every mistake he had made could be rectified if he could keep Gavin from making it. Gavin looked at Evin as a prophet of what he would become in the future. The best version of themselves.

As our plane left the ground in Tampa for our return home after Evin's celebration of life service, Gavin and I experienced a silent moment of immeasurable heaviness. I was afraid it might break us both. But Evin taught us to be stronger than that. We are so thankful for our past, our present, and our future with Evin's wisdom, strength, and love.

~ *Mindy and Gavin Grubbs (Family friends)*

It was Sunday, April 29, 2018. I was back at home in New York, and it was about a month after Evin and I had finished the draft of his book. I woke a little late that morning and saw that I'd gotten a call from Evin's phone the night before. Also, Evin's dad Scott had texted me early in the morning and asked me to call him. I called him as I sat on the edge of my bed, still a little groggy, and he said, "A few days ago, on Thursday, Evin had an accident."

Don't ask me why; I knew what was coming. I leaped up, shouting, "Oh no. Oh, no." I couldn't say more; Scott's voice was even, reassuring, calm, a stalwart pier in a raging sea. "He passed away yesterday," said Scott, even as I was sobbing aloud: No, no, no.

My son Taylor came running into the room and threw his arms around me, not knowing what had happened. Scott explained to me that Evin had been driving his wheelchair in the road Thursday evening, probably too fast, as was his wont, and he ran into a parked car. He broke his ankles and his femur. The emergency room patched him up and sent him home but he was back in the hospital the next day.

"We knew it could happen any time," said Scott as I sobbed, inarticulate. "He had only one lung working; his heart was weak." Evin suffered an embolism as a result of the injuries; a blood clot rose into his lungs and shut down his heart. "He wasn't afraid," said Scott. "He understood what was happening, and he said he was ready to go on." Evin always said he could die any day, but in truth, I didn't believe it. I couldn't imagine it. To be with Evin was to experience a powerful personality, an exuberant and lively spirit. He never seemed weak. For Evin to be gone seemed impossible.

Long moments passed after I hung up the phone until I could speak again, before I could tell Taylor what had happened, or make calls to friends. Taylor knew how close Evin and I had become, but more than that, he understood loss. Not so many years ago, we lost his older brother, my first-born son Spencer, to suicide. Three months later, we lost his father, my husband, also to suicide. The trauma of losing family like this never goes away. Evin and Spencer were about the same age, and I originally decided to help Evin with his book to honor my son's memory.

I'd never known anybody with muscular dystrophy. But strangely enough, just a few months earlier, as the result of a random phone call, I'd become involved with a fundraiser for a local chapter of the Muscular Dystrophy Association. It seemed like a meaningful coincidence. And because I was on my own journey of recovery after the deaths of my son and my husband, Evin's story seemed like a perfect opportunity for me. Evin was just a year older than Spencer. What better way to honor Spencer, who had been studying to be a doctor, than to help another young man with a disability?

Evin's nurse arranged for us to get together at a local Starbucks. I'll never forget that first meeting. I was sitting outside and as I stood, Evin buzzed up in his chair, backed up and neatly came to rest opposite me. The first thing I noticed was that he was handsome; the second was that he was articulate and polite; and the third was that his body was wasted – a sharp contrast to his presence and personality.

I discovered that Evin had already written, with the help of various scribes, about 20 pages of his life story. He was immediately enthusiastic about my helping. We agreed I would scribe for him and then put the story together into a coherent whole. My excitement about the project wasn't merely from the fact that Evin had a unique and important perspective to express. It was the fact that as soon as I met Evin, I really, really liked him. He was wry, sarcastic, and funny. He spoke candidly about his disability, his struggles and his faults. And he didn't hesitate to speak candidly about society's faults, either. After only ten minutes, I knew we could work together.

Not long after we agreed to work on his book, I told Evin I had to meet his parents. I'd be leaving Florida soon, returning to my home in New York. Evin and I planned to talk on the phone regularly, so I could write down his story, then I'd return to Florida for us to work on editing and putting it all together. I could just imagine his parents, with whom he lived, wondering: Who is this lady who all of a sudden is getting into Evin's business?

I spoke to Evin on a regular basis over the phone and typed files and files of his story. Evin tended to pontificate about the meaning of "disabled" versus "handicapped;" rant about the impossibility of being independent if his nurses couldn't drive him places; and complain about minimally handicapped people using the spots where wheelchair vans should go.

I got him to talk to me more about what had actually happened to him. Sometimes I wondered if Evin were exaggerating, or getting it right, and so I thought it would be great to interview other people who had witnessed Evin's life and helped him grow up. Evin thought that was a great idea, too, and he gave me contact information for many of the people who were important in his life. We started visiting and interviewing them for the book, too. It turned out that Evin had not exaggerated, and all of these people added special insights into Evin's story.

We began to go through Evin's life chronologically, and as we did, I realized his story truly was a journey of recovery. Evin's recovery hinged on a desperate despair and depression that overcame him in adolescence, when he began to realize that being disabled was permanent. As he grew up, he realized his peers were not going to treat him like he was just as good as anybody else. He realized he was going to suffer discrimination and humiliation and loneliness because of his disabled body. His life would be filled with hardship and pain. How was he to live with this, much less live well?

That Evin found his answer, and at such a young age, is a marvel. He used to complain about people saying he was an inspiration. He'd get mad and say it wasn't inspirational to just get up and get dressed and go to church. The mothers who got their kids up and got them dressed and got them to church, said Evin, were far more inspirational than he.

But there was this: Evin discovered the true meaning of life in gratitude. He came to embrace every moment, to take every opportunity, to enjoy every laugh, to love every friend. Evin's inspirational secret was that he used everything he was given to get the most out of life, instead of regretting and being angry about what he was not given, instead of laboring under the burden of bitterness. How many times there were that Evin, unwittingly, inspired me to do better in my own journey!

Truly, Evin embraced the diversity of life. He loved to argue, but he never tried to impose. He was a devout Christian, but he never tried to push his faith on others. He was a deeply spiritual and loving man, who despite himself, will always be an inspiration to everyone lucky enough to have known him. I only hope I have done him justice in his book, and that you, the reader, can glimpse a little bit of what it was to have been Evin's friend.

~ Celia Watson Seupel

May 9, 2018

ACKNOWLEDGMENT

The Hartsell Family would like to gratefully acknowledge Celia Watson Seupel, a journalist, poet and writing coach based in New York. While visiting Florida, she heard that a young man with muscular dystrophy was trying to write a memoir and she offered to help. When she and Evin met, they immediately struck up a vibrant friendship. Celia and Evin worked together on his book for two years, sometimes long-distance over the phone, sometimes in person, and we will be forever thankful for her time and efforts in helping Evin write his life story. She has let us know that her deep sadness over the loss of Evin is mingled with a great joy that she was given the gift of knowing Evin in such a deep and meaningful way. You can read more about Celia at *www.CeliaWatsonSeupel.com*.

Evin designed his own business card

ABOUT THE AUTHOR

Evin B. Hartsell was born with Muscular Dystrophy, and during the 28 years of his life he left a positive impression on everyone who knew him. Evin completed this book just two weeks before his passing and in this story he shared his life with the world. Evin loved family, friends, fraternity, and church, and one of the things that mattered most to him was how society tended to judge people with disabilities based on their outward appearance. His desire was that instead of people just seeing his physical disability, they would first look to discover who he really was, and the value of what he could contribute to both them and society. Through his Life's experiences, Evin learned to create a disabled World where he was Abled to help it. His phrase *"Be the Change, Say I Will"* was who he was and how he lived.

A member of the Cub Scouts, Muscular Dystrophy Association State Goodwill Ambassador, Honorary Deputy Sheriff, Honorary Firefighter, High School Chamber Choir, Big Brother Volunteer, Founding Member - Team Phoenix Power Soccer Association, Charter Initiate – Kappa Sigma Fraternity Saint Leo University, Bachelor of Arts in Psychology Saint Leo University, Masters of Business Administration Saint Leo University, Disability Life Coach to All, Master Video Game Player, Marvel Superheroes Subject Matter Expert.

Got an idea for a book? Contact Curry Brothers Publishing, LLC. We are not satisfied until your publishing dreams come true. We specialize in all genres of books, especially religion, leadership, family history, poetry, and children's literature. There's an African Proverb that confirms, "When an elder dies, a library closes." Be careful who tells your family history. Are their values your family's values? Our staff will navigate you through the entire publishing process, and we take pride in going the extra mile in meeting your publishing goals.

Improving the world one book at a time!

Curry Brothers Publishing, LLC
PO Box 247
Haymarket, VA 20168
(719) 466-7518 & (615) 347-9124
Visit us at www.currybrotherspublishing.com